Quick Pickles

Quick Pickles
Easy Recipes with Big Flavor

by Chris Schlesinger, John Willoughby, and Dan George

Photographs by Susie Cushner

CHRONICLE BOOKS

SAN FRANCISCO

Library of Congress Cataloging-in-Publication Data available.
ISBN 0-8118-3015-2
Printed in Hong Kong

The photographer wishes to express sincere gratitude to stylist Helen Crowther,
whose creative vision, focus, and commitment balanced with humor and
perseverance was a consistent force in moving this project forward. I also wish
to thank George Simons for his food styling expertise; Dan George for friendship,
hard work, and great recipes; Sean Hennessey for loyalty and assistance; Chris
Schlesinger and John Willoughby for providing the vehicle, time, and "special"
place; Aaron Dirego and the Back Eddy staff for embracing and feeding us; as
well as Brenda and Chelsy at the Paquachuck Inn; Voyzle at Cosata's Farm stand;
Sara McOsker at Walkers Roadside Stand; and all those whose cooperation and
assistance contributed to the successful completion of this book.

Designed by Yumiko Nakagawa
Typesetting by Jan Martí, Command Z

Distributed in Canada by Raincoast Books
9050 Shaughnessy Street
Vancouver, BC V6P 6E5

10 9 8 7 6 5 4 3 2 1

Chronicle Books LLC
85 Second Street
San Francisco, California 94105
www.chroniclebooks.com

Contents

Acknowledgments

From the three of us:

Our thanks to all the folks at Chronicle Books—first to our editor, Bill LeBlond, for his enthusiasm about quick pickles and the energy, efficiency, and good humor with which he translated our recipes and words into a book; to his assistant, Amy Treadwell, who worked long and cheerfully to keep us on the path to completion; to Pamela Geismar and Yumiko Nakagawa for their vision and skill in designing the book; and to Rebecca Pepper, whose copyediting saved our collective voice while erasing our many collective errors. And of course thanks to Susie Cushner, who took the spectacular photographs that bring our pickles to life in these pages.

Thanks as always to our agent, Doe Coover, for deciding that pickles really were wonderful enough to deserve their own book and for making it happen, and to her colleague Francis, who tirelessly kept us all in touch despite our travels and schedules.

Our thanks also to the entire staff of the Back Eddy for accommodating and supporting the "Pickle Project." In particular, we'd like to thank general manager Sal Liotta, Chef Aaron DeRego, sous chefs Nigel Vincent, Brian Rebello, and Bob DeRego, and assistant general manager Michelle Hough. Thanks also to the Back Eddy wait staff for their voracious, confidence-building pickle appetites and to Maureen Bennett, Back Eddy dessert chef, for resolving the age-old rhubarb pickle dilemma.

Chris Schlesinger
John (Doc) Willoughby
Dan George

And a few more from Dan the Pickle Man:

In addition to the folks acknowledged above, I want to add my personal thanks to James and Nigel for getting me the pickle barrel; to Tim Partridge for his help and encouragement; to Mike Habib, my friend, cooking buddy, and pickle counselor, for loaning me some fine books from his own collection and for providing lots of research and advice; to Jackie Levesque, for being a friend, pickle taster, and ace keyboardist; to my wife, Chris Ash, for surrendering our kitchen and guest room for months on end to a complete pickle invasion; and to Chris and Doc, my co-authors, who gave me the chance to do my thing.

Dan George

Note: A portion of the proceeds from this book have been donated to the Westport Fisherman's Association.

Every cookbook has a story. Some are important, others are meaningful, and still others are funny. I add this story to the list and suggest that it is one of the more unusual, at least in my experience.

The story is set along the southeastern coast of Massachusetts, where the farms run right down to the ocean and if you stand on the beach you can watch the ships of the New Bedford fleet on the home stretch as they enter Buzzard's Bay. The town is Westport, and it very much reminds me of Tidewater, Virginia, where I grew up. So the rural, coastal farming dynamic, with its varied waterways and rich food traditions, is very familiar to me.

Westport is only about an hour south of Cambridge, where I live, and where my original restaurant, the East Coast Grill, is located. For the past fifteen years or so Westport has served as my weekend getaway. There I was able to reconnect with the beach bum tendencies of my youth. Walking with the dogs on the beach, swimming, surfing, fishing, or just lying on the beach with friends having a couple of cold ones occupied most of my time.

During this period I had the good fortune to develop a friendship with a local attorney named Dan George. Not only is Dan a staunch defender of truth and justice, he is also possessed of tremendous cooking skills. I've said many times that Dan is one of the finest natural, nonprofessional cooks that I have ever met.

One of the aspects that solidifies Dan's cooking is his understanding of ingredients. He grows most of his own vegetables in a backyard garden, he knows the best source for Lebanese breads in Fall River, he can tell you where to get the finest chourice in New Bedford, and he has a vast knowledge of the creatures that live in the sea and how to catch them. This last area of expertise provided our friendship with a positive environment for growth—many idle hours spent in an 18-foot boat with a 48-horsepower motor pursuing the striped bass and its relatives. When we weren't hauling out big lunkers, we daydreamed about different fun ingredients, great meals we'd had, and restaurants we'd like to open.

Strangely enough, the last daydream actually came to fruition. In April of 1999 I opened the Back Eddy, a restaurant right on the east branch of the Westport River, overlooking historic Westport Point and presiding over choice seats for summer sunsets. Dan was the one who came up with the name. His logic was not only that a "back eddy" is a current that flows counter to the mainstream, which is always a good thing to be a part of, but also that there is an actual physical back eddy that occurs twice daily in front of the restaurant one hour after high tide.

That spring, with the restaurant due to open in three weeks, Dan told me he was reconsidering his relationship to the law and began to express a desire to try his amateur cooking hand in a more professional setting. Of course, I was more than willing to hire him on, but the chef was kind of overwhelmed with his opening responsibilities and was not really in a position to mentor a seriously inspired but still green newcomer. So he asked me if I might find a job that Dan could do for a couple of weeks, until he could catch up and be in a better position to direct Dan's talents.

That was no problem. I knew that not only was Dan a quick study, but he also had an excellent conceptual understanding of flavor that he seemed to have been born with. I decided to take advantage of these qualities and harness Dan's enthusiasm to pursue what had long been a culinary interest of mine. I had always been fascinated by the pickles of the world, but my interest was not always shared by my fellow chefs, so I saw an opportunity to expand the Back Eddy's pickle profile. On that day in April 1999, I anointed Dan as what I suspect to be the country's first official Pickle Chef. I mean, there are dessert chefs, fish chefs, salad chefs, so why not a chef who specializes in pickles?

Because Westport is a farming community, I thought it would be a nice gesture to serve our customers a complimentary dish of pickles as soon as they sat down at their tables. I gave Dan the assignment of creating them, along with my grandmother's recipe for classic bread-and-butter pickles. The second time Dan made the recipe he asked if it was all right to make a couple of modifications, which actually improved the pickle (sorry, Grandma).

The next day Dan brought in some rhubarb with an idea for a pickle that I found a little odd, but I told him to go ahead. He proceeded to create his Rhubarb Pickles with Caramelized Onions, which caught not only my attention but that of the wait staff and the diners when we sent it out as an accompaniment to those other harbingers of spring, soft-shelled crab and shad roe. It was a dead-on hit.

At that point I bought Dan a couple of books that described the wonderful pickle traditions of India. In a few days he had produced Mango Pickle with Scorched Mustard Seed. My friend and co-author, Doc (also known as John Willoughby), who is also a big fan of pickles, happened to stop by Dan's house at about that point. When he tasted the mango pickles, he couldn't get enough of them. He also couldn't stop talking about them, telling everyone he ran into about this incredible flavor combination and the lawyer/cook who had created it.

By this time Dan was fully ignited. His next area of endeavor was Korean kimchee. Not content just to read about it, he went to the home of his friend Morea Kim to learn her family's pickling secrets. Customers also started to share their pickle experiences with Dan, which lead him to the Eastern European pickle mecca of

Gus's Pickles in New York. Inspired by this visit, he acquired a wine barrel from our neighbors at Westport Rivers Vineyards and made a batch of Kick-Ass Barrel Cukes, which quickly became a Back Eddy favorite.

Doc and I were now fully re-engaged with our longtime infatuation with condiments in general and pickles in particular. When our literary agent, Doe Coover, visited the Back Eddy, tasted Dan's pickles, and listened to us rave about how many culinary uses there were for these little gems, she decided a book was in order. And here it is.

So that's the story. Since then the legend of Dan the Pickle Man has continued to grow. When I got married, he provided the immensely popular pickle bar—requested by my wife, Marcy, a longtime pickle connoisseur—at the reception. That same pickle bar wowed cookbook authors and food journalists at a luncheon during the convention of the International Association of Culinary Professionals in Providence last spring.

The bottom line is that this book is a story of a person's love of food and of how preparing and sharing food can bring out the best in all of us. Dan's intense enthusiasm for pickles is both contagious and inspiring. The joy with which he approaches the subject is wonderful to be a part of, both for me and for Doc. We hope you enjoy it, too.

Chris Schlesinger
June 2000

Hot Peppers
50 bs/c.

Homemade pickles have it all: they taste fantastic, they've got that great crunch, they're an ideal snack, they can set up all kinds of main dishes, they have strong and interesting flavors, they're an unintimidating way to sample the flavor footprints of the world—and besides all that, they're good for you.

Okay, you might say, but what about all the hassle? What about the boiling water baths and the rubber sealers and tin lids for the jars, and the fear that if you don't follow a precise procedure you might poison yourself and all your friends?

Well, you can forget all that. Because what we're talking about in this book are "quick pickles." And we really do mean quick; many go from garden or produce stand to pickle perfection in just a couple of hours. Meant to remain refrigerated for a few weeks or months until eaten, these quick pickles have the flavor, tang, and snap of old-fashioned pickles without the labor or the fear. As an added benefit, they also have a freshness often missing from traditional long-stored pickles.

To our minds, these modern pickles are the latest in a beneficial culinary evolution that started long ago. As almost everybody knows, the process of pickling originated as a form of preservation. In the centuries before mechanical refrigeration, the magical ability of salt brines and acids to defer spoilage provided a very important means of extending the harvest. In a happy coincidence, the resulting pickles also served an important culinary role, adding bright, deep, intense flavors to meals that could otherwise be monotonous. So it's not surprising that pickles were beloved throughout most of the world, with each country and region adding its own signature spices and flavorings. From the pickled ginger of Japan to the pickled turnips of Lebanon and the pickled chile peppers of South America, pickles enlivened almost every cuisine.

In this, as in many other things, the United States inherited traditions from all over the world. And since pickles were at once so practical and so popular, until the middle of the twentieth century virtually every home cook in this country was a practiced pickler. Certainly all three of us have deep pickle memories, uniformly based on the skills of our grandmothers.

Doc grew up in a small town in Iowa, and his Grandmother Schwyhart, who had lived all her life on a farm, was a fiend for pickling. A meal at her house was not complete without at least one kind of pickle, and often several, brought up from the rows and rows arrayed on shelves in the basement. When the county fair took place down at the fairgrounds each year, Doc was always puzzled that his grandmother was more interested in who took first prize in the pickling contest than in the hoopla surrounding the other events, but now he definitely gets it. After all, if you spent much of your adult life raising and preserving all of your own food in the absence of electricity or running water, you naturally developed a deep appreciation for a fine hand at pickling. And those were some pickles.

Chris's first pickle memories involve arguing with his older sister, Susan, about who would get the last sweet pickle in the canning jar at his Grandmother Wetzler's. These pickles were so coveted that even later in life Chris and his sister would argue vociferously about how many jars each of them should get from the seasonal shipments. Even the brine was prized for use in chicken, tuna, or egg salads. But they were only one among the many pickles that graced Grandma Wetzler's table. She had a large garden, and during the season she would "put up" all the excess produce. The giant bowls of salted vegetables, the big pots of brine, and the very dangerous and terribly interesting sterilization process are all part of Chris's pickle memories.

Now picture Dan's Lebanese-American household in Brockton, Massachusetts, on a summer Saturday back in the 1940s. Home from a week of work in the shoe factory, his grandfather would preside over the harvesting of produce from the backyard garden. Neighbors would gather, men mostly, to talk in Arabic and English, to supervise, and occasionally even to help. Eventually, Dan's grandmother or mother would bring out a sweating pitcher of ice water and some snacks—the *mezze* tray. Prominent among the triangles of flatbread topped with charred herbs, the fresh white cheeses, the dishes of hummus, the wedged tomatoes and cucumbers, and the leftover spinach pies would be stuffed pickled grape leaves, several kinds of brined olives (which after all are really a pickle), and—pickle pièce de résistance—a dish of Day-Glo fuchsia pickled turnips, sparkling in both color and flavor.

It is no accident that in each of our cases our pickle memories were supplied by an earlier generation, because modern refrigeration and transportation have made it unnecessary to preserve food as our forebears did. That's clearly a good thing, but an unfortunate by-product is that the practice of home pickling has all but died out in this country. Nevertheless, we still crave the distinctive sweet-tart flavor of pickles, just as we love the flavors of ham and bacon, both of which originally resulted from the need to preserve meat but are now eaten for their taste alone.

To get the wonderful flavors of pickles, people have turned to less-than-optimal commercial products. To most modern Americans, pickles are born in jars. But quick pickles can change all of that. Because now, with little fuss and no fear, you can make pickles that satisfy your taste buds while also providing a connection with the hands-on era that seems to be fading away. You really can have it both ways: near-instant gratification that you create yourself.

You'll also find that these homemade pickles are wonderful to have around the house. For one thing, they are a stand-out healthful snack. Mind you, we're not snack snobs. On any given day you might find us munching on anything from potato chips to pretzels to cheese puffs. But when the big game is on or special guests are coming over, we're most likely to bring out the pickles. They are uniquely intriguing, and they make everybody happy because, without having to pay any fat penalty, you get satisfying crunch and intense flavor at the same time.

Pickles are also a key resource for the dinner table. Their potent flavors lend staunch culinary support in the form of dazzling contrast to something more prominent on the plate, such as meat or fish. To us, this means that the flavor of a pickle should not be subdued but instead must be tangy, bright, and forceful.

We always knew that pickles needed these qualities, but as we worked on the recipes in this book the true inner nature of pickles became more and more clear to us. The issue cropped up, for example, when Dan made his first version of the Corn, Cucumber, and Chile Pickle. It was late July, and Dan was desperate for the clean, sweet flavor of the very first ears of native corn. So he stirred up a big batch using the kernels from about a dozen ears, flavored them with a modest amount of vinegar and a little toasted cumin, and ate about half of it before it cooled. Then he made another batch that had a strong vinegary taste more typical of pickles and was assertively flavored with ginger, mustard, and garlic. After a few belts of the punchy blend, he went back to the milder pickle, confident in its superiority.

When Dan presented his clear favorite to his cooking teammates, they liked it—well, sort of. After a bit of hemming and hawing, they said it tasted too much like a salad. Dan reluctantly let them try the stronger one, and it was all over; it was the unanimous winner over the more mellow offering.

The perspective of Dan's cohorts was that pickles exist to charge the palate, in sharp contrast to other, "rounder" flavored foods like meats, fish, rice, and beans. That in turn means that a pickle's punch should not be pulled. Otherwise it becomes something else: a salad, where the vegetable stars and the vinaigrette fades to a supporting role. After trying the more aggressively flavored version of this pickle next to a serving of grilled native scallops, Dan came over to the true flavor side, where he remains to this day.

We learned many other lessons, too, in the course of working on what we came to call our Pickle Project. Many had to do with other people's pickle traditions, their importance in family life, and what they could tell us about cultural attitudes. For instance, Dan had never tasted, let alone made, kimchee until he began this pickle pilgrimage. So Dan went to our friend Steve Johnson, who'd been trying out kimchees for about two years at the Blue Room, his restaurant in Cambridge, Massachusetts. Steve said that although some Koreans who had come into the restaurant and tried his quick kimchee (which is truly delicious) had given it unqualified compliments, much of the response was more on the order of "Not bad for a white man." After talking to Steve, Dan began to wonder if making kimchee was doomed to be like making Cajun gumbo, a pursuit at which outsiders automatically fail and insiders constantly quibble.

In this case, as in most others, Dan decided to go to the source. So he turned to his Korean friend, Morea Kim, asking her to show him how to make kimchee the way her grandmother did. She agreed, and one sunny Sunday she arrived at Dan's house bearing bundles of fresh ingredients from her favorite store. She explained that the gathering of just the right ingredients was as much a part of the

November harvest ritual back home as that of making, packing, and burying the kimchee underground in crocks for the winter ahead.

As Morea carefully pried the cabbages open along their delicate folds and ruffles, she nostalgically recalled the hands and faces of the women in her life as they put this recipe together, while the men dug holes for the crocks' annual burial in their garden. And as she very carefully scattered sea salt among the cabbage leaves, Morea remembered how her grandmom would sleep with one eye open, waiting to rinse the salted cabbage sections at just the right moment of wilting. With perhaps the most animation of all, she described how, as a little girl, she would be sent outside in winter to get some kimchee for the meal. Crimping her fingers like a woodchuck at its burrow, Morea demonstrated how she would need to claw a little at the icy surface of the kimchee crock to get at the buried treasure. But she also told how it was "Oh, so good" once retrieved, and she gloried in memories of her joy and pride at bringing it indoors to her waiting family. If kimchee was not on the table, she said, her dad would not consider the table to be set.

As we absorbed pickle lore, we also learned that the pickled turnips and cucumbers and cabbage of yore weren't for everyone. Those pickles often had a harsh, salty attitude, having just done hard time in a strong vinegar and salt solution down in the cellar. After World War II, when the hot water bath and canning process became more widespread, the quantities of salt and vinegar in pickles decreased and the flavor became milder. We think that we

have taken the next logical step with the fresher, milder, somewhat fruitier quick pickles in this book.

Despite their differences, though, the same basic dynamics are at work in our quick pickles as in more traditional long-stored versions. So let's look at how each of the three types of pickles in this book are made.

How Pickles Work

Pickles basically fall into one of three camps: fresh, fermented, and oil-preserved. Most of the pickles in this book are quick and easy fresh pickles. But we've also included a handful of recipes for fermented pickles, which, although they involve a bit more time and attention, are really fun to make and have beautiful flavors and aromas. The oil pickles that are so popular in parts of Asia are also among our favorites for their compellingly exotic flavors.

We'll start with the pickle types that most of us are familiar with: fresh and fermented. The two defining ingredients in these pickles are, respectively, vinegar and salt. Let's look at fresh pickles first, since they constitute the majority of the pickles in this book.

Fresh Pickles: The Crunch Factor

Both fresh and fermented pickles are preserved—or, in the case of the quick pickles in this book, flavored—with acid, usually in the form of some kind of vinegar. The science involved is very simple indeed: most microbes (that is to say, bacteria and their ilk) just can't grow in a high-acid environment, so spoilage is severely retarded, almost stopped. However, while fermented pickles need to make their own acid over time through the fermentation process, acid is added to fresh pickles right from the beginning, most often in the form of vinegar or citrus.

Like their fermented brethren, these fresh pickles also contain salt. In fact, in the quick pickles we're making here, the salt is just as important as the vinegar. It's crucial to the all-important crunch factor. When you let a fruit or vegetable—or any food, really—sit in contact with salt, a strange dichotomy occurs: the food wilts and at the same time becomes crunchy, two conditions usually considered to be opposites.

The reason for this apparent contradiction is simple: salt has a tendency to replace the liquid in anything with which it comes into contact. Salt not only draws out the fluid that is already free inside the food in question—what we think of as the "juice"—but also causes some of the protein molecules in the food to denature (unwind), freeing some of the liquid that was bound up inside these molecules. The salt then draws this liquid out of the food as well. While this unwinding phenomenon is much more pronounced in meat or fish, it also occurs to some extent in vegetables.

With some of its moisture removed, a vegetable or fruit will contract just a bit, so that it looks wilted, sometimes even wrinkled. But that same loss of water makes it crisp and crunchy, rather than flabby and soft, as it would be if it had lost its water through slow evaporation rather than salt-induced extraction.

This same phenomenon also explains one of the reasons that pickles, after sitting in their pickling solution for rel-atively short periods of time, can become so nicely flavored all the way through. Having lost their moisture, fruits and vegetables get thirsty. When they are put into a pickling syrup, they eagerly soak it up, which gets the flavor right down into them.

An added advantage of salting fresh pickles is that the action of the salt in drawing out the liquid concentrates and intensifies the inherent flavor of the food in much the same way that sun-drying does.

Because we don't intend to preserve these pickles for long storage, we don't need to worry about drawing out a lot of moisture. We want to remove only enough to help the vegetables stay crunchy and to intensify their natural flavors a bit. Even so, we had to deal with the twin issues of time and taste when figuring out how long our pickles-to-be should interact with salt. Since ours are quick recipes, we generally came down on the side of minimal salting times, in most cases only an hour or so. If you want more crunch, let your fruits and vegetables sit longer.

You could also intensify the crunch by using more salt, but we found that this adversely affected the flavor of the pickles. It also required proportionately more rinsing or even soaking to get rid of the excess salt. So our recipes often call for adding moderate amounts of salt, draining off the salty liquid that results from the salt's action, and then rinsing the fruit or vegetable once or twice "to taste." In the case of certain durable vegetables, we have added a squeeze after the draining, which gets out a little more water and makes an even crunchier pickle.

Heat is also a factor in preserving crunch. In the old days, when preservation was a paramount issue, fruits and vegetables were sometimes fully cooked before being pickled. There is no need to do this with the quick pickles we're talking about here, but you still have to deal with the effects of heat.

The traditional approach to fresh pickles is to put the fruit or vegetables in the acidified syrup, bring the mixture to a boil, and then turn off the heat. In fact, that was how Dan started out making his pickles when he first attained his position as official Pickle Chef at the Back Eddy restaurant. But we very quickly discovered that this is not really the best approach for home cooks, or at least for relatively relaxed and inexact cooks like us. Distracted by other activities in the busy kitchen, Dan wasn't mindful enough of the simmering mixture and let it go for a bit longer than the two minutes he intended. As you might guess, the pickles were too soft. Without their crunch they just weren't as satisfying as we wanted them to be, so we eventually chopped them up and mixed them into a relish.

After several such experiences, we decided that a method that requires rather strict adherence to time limits was not for us. So for our pickles we chose another approach: bringing the acidified syrup to a boil separately and then pouring it over the fruit or vegetables either hot or at room temperature. This conveniently eliminates the risk of overcooking without requiring you to keep an eagle eye on the stove—and convenience and lack of requirements are very big with us.

Fermented Pickles: Fruit of the Brine
Fermented pickles are the aristocrats of the pickle world. As such, they require a bit more time, attention, and fussing over than fresh pickles. But they are fascinating to make, they really aren't difficult, and they have many subtle nuances of flavor. We couldn't resist including some.

It's not at all surprising that fermented pickles have complex, nuanced flavors. They share this trait with other products of fermentation, such as wine, soy sauce, sourdough bread, and cheese.

Although it produces complicated flavors, fermentation is actually a pretty straightforward process. Basically, what you are doing is creating an environment in which certain beneficial microbes found in the atmosphere multiply, while others—the ones that cause spoilage—are kept at bay. In the case of pickles, the microbes we are looking for are bacteria (as opposed to, for example, yeast). As these bacteria go to work, they create many flavorful by-products, one of which is lactic acid. Like the vinegar in fresh pickles, the lactic acid helps preserve the fruit or vegetable. Salt is the agent responsible for keeping unwanted microbes out of the action as fermentation takes off. So these pickles start off by being either mixed with salt, as in Morea Kim's Grandmother's Stuffed Cabbage Kimchee, or immersed in a salt brine, as in Kick-Ass Westport River Barrel Cukes.

That's the fermentation process in a nutshell. But how exactly do you make a fermented pickle? What happens during the process? It seems mysterious—and actually it is a little mysterious, because fermentation is a bit like alchemy—but it is very simple, too.

The first step is to put the pickles-to-be into the container in which they're going to ferment. Any nonreactive container will do the trick here: crocks, bowls, jars, whatever you choose. But you might want to select a clear glass container for its display qualities. In that department, the absolute best option is a jar with a mouth large enough to put your hand in followed by wider "shoulders." The shoulders will pin the pickling vegetables down so they don't bob to the surface as easily.

If you do use a glass jar, you can start, as Dan does, by arranging the raw materials as you would a floral display. This is a lot easier to do when the glass is dry. First to go into the jar is the primary ingredient—the main fruit or vegetable—which Dan likes to pack in vertically. Then you can slide the showier ingredients around the sides. The result is a beautiful display, with lacy dill fronds or bright pink peppercorns or snowy fresh horseradish or beautiful concentric white circles of onions plastered against the glass, as if you were looking into an aquarium. Grape leaves are also great for this, and they also contain a chemical that helps maintain the crunch of the pickles.

If you do start the process by arranging your ingredients in this fashion, don't be surprised to find guests asking how to make these beautiful floral-type displays for their own homes. But this type of display is certainly not essential; after all, the point of these pickles is their flavor. To get that, you need to begin simply by placing the ingredients into a nonreactive container. At that point you pour the brine, which is nothing more than salt and water plus some flavorings, into the container, making sure that everything is immersed. (This has the pleasant side effect of making the ingredients even more vivid and bright, like stones in water.) Now you cover the container with a piece of cheesecloth or a clean cotton cloth and set it where it can rest for a few days.

That's the hard part. Now it's just a matter of watching, sampling, and enjoying. Or, as Dan puts it, you "Wait, watch, smell, sample, admire, gloat, eat."

The rate of fermentation is determined primarily by the saltiness of the brine and the temperature of the room. The ideal temperature is in the mid- to high 60s, so if you are making these pickles in the dead of summer you might want to set them in a cool room.

What happens next? On the first day nothing much. On the second day you may see a bubble or two rising to the surface or forming on one of the submerged ingredients. You will also start to notice a wonderful aroma wafting out of the pickle container. Indeed, it's going to smell so great that we recommend you make a little extra brine when you first fill the container because you may well want to begin sipping it at this point.

On the third day you will probably see some bubbles rising to the surface, and you'll also notice the color of the vegetables starting to fade ever so slightly. There still won't be a lot of bubbles on the top, but if you give the jar wall a slight tap you may set a few bubbles free, which is cause for rejoicing because the magic is starting to happen.

By the fourth day a lot should be happening in your pickle jar, with enough bubbles coming to the surface to form a kind of foam. Once a day from now until you declare the pickle finished, you should skim the bubbles from the surface of the liquid with a spoon, just as you would skim the foam from something you are boiling. This takes about five seconds, but it's important that you do it every day.

That's all you have to do, other than deciding when the pickles are done, which is pretty much up to you because, like all foods, pickles are personal. What you are looking for is the point at which the saltiness and sweetness you began with is balanced by the eventual sourness and penetration/ripening/melding of other flavors to the degree that you personally prefer.

For most people's taste buds, that point is reached somewhere around the time fermentation stops, particularly with these quick-fermenting pickles. It usually stops after five to six days; you'll know when it's done because bubbles will stop rising to the surface. Of course, you may prefer your pickles a little milder or sweeter, in which case you can refrigerate the pickles at any point after the first day you skim foam. (It's not worth doing it before that, because you won't get any of the advantages of fermentation.) Remember, the brine will continue to penetrate and flavor the pickles even though the fermentation has ended

Once the pickles have achieved the flavor you like, simply cover and refrigerate them, and you've got delicious fermented pickles, ready to go. Now how hard was that?

We do have to add one word of caution. If you open your pickle container and find that your pickles have turned slippery and mushy, toss them out. This means that unde-

sirable microbes have somehow grown, and you definitely don't want to be eating them. This has never happened to us, and it is unlikely to happen with these pickles that are quickly fermented and then refrigerated, but it's better to be safe than sorry.

We hope we've convinced you that making fermented pickles is not a big deal, because we know you'll enjoy it if you try. In addition to their intricate flavors, these pickles also provide the joy of alchemy, of participation in a display of nature's transformative power. Each batch is an experiment that, once launched, takes on a life of its own. Waiting for the three-day bubbles to appear is like looking for the first sprouts after you have planted seeds, and you sure can't get that joy of metamorphosis by opening a jar.

Oil Pickles: Almost Totally Tropical

The pickles that are least familiar to most Americans are those made with oil. But oil is an excellent preservative, and it is particularly useful in tropical countries. Oil does not preserve by chemical action, as do salt and acid, but rather by the simple mechanism of sealing the pickle off from air. In the old days many cooks, even in America, topped off their fermented or fresh pickles with a layer of oil, just for good measure.

Because oil preserves in a mechanical rather than a chemical fashion, it does not add as much flavor to the mix as other preservation methods. But cooks in hot countries have dealt with this simply by adding flavorings to the oil. In Italy, a pickle maker might take an especially tasty olive oil and infuse it with garlic, pepper, and herbs such as rosemary, thyme, bay leaf, basil, and oregano. But the world headquarters of oil pickles is India, which also happens to be, in our opinion, the country where spices are used most expertly and imaginatively. The typical Indian way of flavoring oil pickles is to infuse vegetable oils with a carefully chosen array of spices and chiles, typically in a hot skillet. Flavor options and combinations are many, and we took advantage of these in some of the recipes we developed for this book.

We also used a couple of other techniques to enlarge the flavors of our oil pickles. In some instances, we introduced the smoky flavor of the grill to vegetables before pickling them. A second approach was a bit more iconoclastic. Most traditional oil pickles lack an acidic component, which means they are missing an important dimension of the "big flavor" notion that we like to have working in our pickles. When we tried to introduce acid into these pickles along with the oil, we found that it had little effect. It turns out that oil tends to seal the surface of fruits and vegetables, keeping other flavors from penetrating easily. So we decided to try marinating the fruits and vegetables in a little bit of citrus juice or vinegar before adding the pickling oil. We think it works pretty well, giving these pickles a tang that they otherwise would have lacked.

Another characteristic of oil pickles is that they are not quite as "quick" as fresh pickles, largely due to the oil's tendency to slow down flavor penetration. This is not really a problem, because the oil pickles in this book all taste great and have nice, crunchy texture in their infancy. But

despite our usual impatience, we have found that it is worth waiting for the flavors to mellow and penetrate and for the fruits to soften. We couldn't believe what huge, delicious changes occurred in these pickles over a month or so of sitting in (or even out of) the refrigerator.

Oil pickles require a couple other minor tasks. During the first week or so that they are refrigerated, it helps to give them a shake or stir every day or two so the oil stays evenly distributed. Also, because olive oil congeals somewhat at refrigerator temperatures, any pickles that use this oil need to come back to room temperature before you eat them.

Finally, whatever you do, don't throw out any leftover oil when the pickles are gone. It has hundreds of uses: it's fantastic drizzled onto grilled bread, fresh mozzarella, salad greens, grilled or steamed vegetables, pasta, or just about anything else you can think of. Like the brine of fresh and fermented pickles, it's an added benefit that you don't want to lose.

Pickle Purposes

It's no great mystery how to use pickles. They make great snacks and sensational accompaniments to main dishes of all descriptions. But we figured that since we have tasted all of these pickles many times and used them in a range of culinary situations, it might be helpful if we made some suggestions. So in most of the recipes we have given you some pointers as to the use (or uses) that we liked best for that particular pickle. Please don't let our suggestions stop you from expressing your own culinary creativity and using the pickle in any way that seems interesting to you, however.

At the end of this book you'll find a group of recipes that we have called "Pantry Pickles." With the exception of the Purple Pickled Eggs, which are there mainly because they are a kind of oddity, these are pickles that have a multiplicity of uses in everyday cooking, as sort of all-purpose condiments. If you have some of these on hand, your meals never have to be dull.

In some recipes we have also given you ideas for using the pickle brine. This is something that many people seem not to have thought about, but for centuries pickle brines have been put to many uses, from skin conditioner to soup stock to healthful tonic. This practice is not just a relic of the past, either. Not long ago, when Doc was in Istanbul, he visited a store devoted solely to handmade pickles. After he had sampled five or six varieties, each better than the last, the owner took him across the store to what looked like a soda fountain counter. There the proud proprietor filled a glass from one of those aerators that they serve lemonade from in the United States, and he handed it to Doc. It was pickle brine, of course, and it was very tasty, like thin V-8 with a powerful vinegar punch. Even if you don't want to drink brine, consider adding it to salads, using it as a poaching medium for fish, or taking us up on some of the other suggestions we make throughout the book. You won't regret it.

We also want to encourage you to substitute other fruits and vegetables in our recipes. Our selection is purely personal, although there is a rationale behind it. Since the inspiration for this book came from the fields, forests, and rivers of Westport on the southern coast of Massachusetts, most of the fruits and vegetables are ones that are readily available in that region. We do believe, after all, in using local seasonal produce whenever we can. But there are also some tropical fruits and vegetables, from mangoes to jicama, that make such delicious pickles (and that are available in such good quality these days) that we couldn't resist including them.

The Last Word: No Fear

If you're like us, you like to cook spontaneously and largely just for fun. That means you probably have some idea in the back of your mind that pickling means canning and chemistry, that it is complicated and risky. So did we. But in the course of working on this book we learned to discard caution and find the Pickler Within. It took us a while to shake the notion that with this loose attitude we were violating Nature somehow or betraying an unforgiving cult. We found, however, that there were no retributions and plenty of rewards.

It is our hope that this book will bring you back to the idea of home pickling, but without the work and the fear of failure. It could be that, before long, when someone talks about being "in a pickle," you'll think they're bragging instead of complaining. In fact, after making just one recipe, we think you'll understand Dan's personal pickle motto: "No heavy lifting, just bliss."

Rather than proceeding alphabetically, as is the custom, we're going to start our glossary with the two most important ingredients: salt and vinegar. The reason for this is simple: it's crucial to know about both of these ingredients if you're going to be doing quick pickling. After that, you'll find an alphabetical list of some of the less common ingredients found in this book.

Salt of the earth (or the sea):

Not so long ago, we thought that salt was just salt. Why make a fuss about it? But over the past few years we have learned that it is worth understanding the differences among the many types of salt. As a general rule, we prefer kosher or other coarse types of salt. Here are some specifics.

Table salt, which is what most of us grew up with, is a very finely ground refined salt that usually includes iodine and always contains additives to make it free flowing. There is nothing wrong with it per se, but there's not much to be said in its favor either. Its primary virtue seems to be that it flows easily through the holes in salt shakers. We recommend that you not use it for pickling, because it sometimes develops "off" flavors.

Kosher salt, a coarser salt with no additives, is our salt of preference for general cooking as well as pickling. We think it tastes better than table salt, plus its larger crystals seem to stick to food better. Even more important, these larger crystals are more fun to sprinkle onto food with your fingers. When it comes to pickling, we prefer kosher salt for its flavor and because it seems to dissolve more cleanly into liquid. If you choose to use table salt rather than kosher, though, you should be aware that, because of its larger crystals, kosher salt contains about 30 to 50 percent less actual salt by weight than the same volume of table salt. So, for example, if a recipe calls for 2 tablespoons of kosher salt, you should use only about 1 tablespoon of table salt.

Pickling salt is simply fine-grained salt similar to table salt, but with no additives. It dissolves quickly and is perfectly fine for use in any of these recipes. As with table salt, though, you should use roughly half the amount that is called for in our recipes.

Sea salt is a generic term for salt that has been gathered by evaporation from sea water rather than by mining deposits from ancient seas. Sea salts are usually quite expensive and may be green, gray, black, or pink rather than white. Most are intensely "salty," and many have other mild but distinctive flavor overtones. They are very appropriate for some pickles, particularly Asian varieties. But before using sea salt in a pickle, we advise you to taste the particular variety and be sure that its flavor seems compatible with the other ingredients.

Vinegars:

Along with salt, vinegars are essential to quick pickling. Vinegars are created by a double fermentation process. During the first part of the process, sugars in liquids like apple juice and grape juice are turned to alcohol; in the second part, yeast cells are introduced into the liquid, and they turn the alcohol to acetic acid, which gives you vinegar. There are many kinds of vinegars, with different flavors and levels of acid. Most of the vinegars listed here have an acid level of about 5 percent. The exceptions are balsamic, which tends to be higher, around 6 percent, and rice wine vinegar, which is closer to 4 percent.

Apple cider vinegar: Quite popular for its earthy flavor, this vinegar is made from fermented apple cider.

Balsamic vinegar: Balsamic is a mellow, complex, distinctly flavored red wine vinegar. True balsamic is aged in wooden casks, and the contents of several different casks are combined during the aging process to create the final product. This time-consuming process makes true balsamic not only much more complex and tasty but also much more expensive than the version found in most supermarkets. It is wonderful for drizzling onto fruit or greens or for adding a touch of flavor to a wide range of dishes. For the volume you will use in quick pickles, though, you'll probably want to buy one of the cheaper varieties—but do taste it to be sure it actually has good flavor. Beware of those that are harsh or overly sweet.

Homemade vinegars: If you are one of those people who like to make their own vinegars, this is the book for you. Most homemade vinegars have significantly less than the 5 percent acid required to prevent microbial growth in traditional long-stored pickles, but they are perfect for our quick pickles, providing plenty of handmade flavor without any harshness.

Red wine vinegar: The name says it all—it's made from red wine. It varies wildly in quality, depending on the wine and the aging process used. The most expensive red wine vinegars are aged in wooden vats.

Rice vinegar, also known as rice wine vinegar: The Asian version of red wine vinegar, this is made from fermented rice water and has a beautifully delicate, subtle taste.

Sherry vinegar: This is simply vinegar made from sherry. As you might expect, it has a somewhat richer, nuttier, more complex flavor than vinegars made from nonfortified wines.

White, or distilled white, vinegar: Like vodka, this garden-variety vinegar is made from grains. It is the least subtle of vinegars, made through a quick distillation process.

White wine vinegar: Like red wine vinegar, but made from white wine.

Allspice berries: These are the dried, unopened but mature beans of an evergreen tree native to the Caribbean. Slightly larger than peppercorns, the reddish beans have an aromatic flavor that is slightly on the sour side. Many folks think that they taste like a combination of cinnamon, cloves, and nutmeg with a sort of peppery background, hence the name allspice.

Anchovy paste: A combination of mashed anchovies, vinegar, spices, and water, this product usually comes in a tube. It can be substituted in pickle recipes for other salty fish products such as fish sauce.

Cardamom: A sweet, aromatic spice, cardamom is a member of the ginger family and the second most expensive spice in the world (after saffron). There are three varieties of cardamom—green, white, and brown—but the white pods are actually just bleached green ones. Either white or green cardamom is preferable to the brown, which is considerably less aromatic and perfumey. You can buy cardamom in seed form, but you'll get a fuller flavor if you buy it in the pods and then extract the little dark brown or black seeds yourself. It's very easy—simply split open the papery pod with your fingernail and pull out the seeds. When using cardamom in quick pickles, it's a good idea to crush the seeds slightly so their flavor disseminates into the pickling liquid more quickly.

Chile peppers: These fiery little pods, members of the *Capsicum* genus, are the featured New World contribution to spice cookery. After their "discovery" by the Europeans who came to the Americas in the fifteenth century, chiles spread around the globe, becoming inextricably entwined in the cuisines of many countries. The varieties of chiles are many and bewildering—red, green, fresh, dried, super-hot, sweet, you name it. Since there are more than two thousand chile varieties, each with its own heat level and individual flavor, we don't often call for a particular variety. Instead, we recommend that you locate a variety that you enjoy and that is readily available in your area and then develop a relationship with it. That way you will get to know just how hot a dish will be if you add a certain amount of your favorite chile.

Chinese cabbage: Known as "celery cabbage" because of its mild taste and crunchy texture, this cabbage is a staple in northern China and is used in pickled form all over Asia. The two varieties most widely available in the United States are napa, which has an oval, barrel-shaped head, and Michihli (named after a bay in northern China), which is longer and more cylindrical.

Chipotles: Chipotles, which are dried, smoked jalapeño chile peppers, are flat and wrinkled, with a dark reddish brown color; they are about 1 to 1 1/2 inches long. Chipotles have a unique, smoky, imposing flavor that goes with everything, and (particularly important for novice chile users) they have a consistent level of heat. They are usually found canned in adobo sauce, a mixture of vinegar, onions, tomatoes, and spices. However, you may also find them dried.

Coriander seed: Like the leaves and stems (commonly known as cilantro), the small, yellow-brown seeds of the

How about "Pickling Spices"?

A certain combination of aromatic spices is so popular in pickle making that the mixture is sold in prepackaged form as "pickling spices." The exact composition varies somewhat from one manufacturer to another, but common choices include mustard seed, peppercorns, celery seed, coriander seed, cloves, cinnamon, allspice berries, ginger, and bay leaves. You can either make your own (see page 37 for one version) or buy it prepackaged from a market. In either case, it's a good idea to shake the mixture before you use it, since the larger (and therefore heavier) pieces tend to work their way toward the bottom of whatever container the spices are in, meaning that an unshaken pour from that container will be heavily weighted in favor of the smaller spices.

coriander plant are widely used in Asian and Latin cooking. Lightly toasted and ground to a powder, the fruity, warm, spicy, flowery seeds are an essential ingredient in curry powders as well as many chutneys and sambals. Toasting whole coriander seeds just before using them brings out their flavor and aroma.

Cumin seed: These greenish yellow "seeds," with their distinctive, nutty flavor, are actually the ripe fruit of an annual herb of the same name. They are an integral part of the cooking of India and are also widely used in Latin, African, and Middle Eastern cuisines. Their taste is similar to their cousin caraway, but more musty. There is also a black variety of cumin, which has a sweeter, more refined, and more complex flavor, but it is expensive and difficult to locate. As with other spice seeds, toasting cumin prior to use really brings out its flavor and aroma.

Daikon: This is a very large Asian radish with a fresh, sweet flavor. Its skin may be white or black, but the flesh of both types is white, crisp, and juicy. The most popular vegetable in Japan, it makes an excellent, particularly crispy pickle.

Fennel seed: The dried seed of a perennial herb, fennel has a flavor resembling licorice with a slightly bitter aftertaste. The plant from which it comes is similar in appearance to celery and has a fainter but fresher licorice taste. The fronds, stalks, and bulb are all also used in cooking.

Fenugreek: This spice is the seed of an annual herb of the pea family. The seeds look like tiny nuggets, and their flavor when ground is slightly sweet and spicy, but mainly bitter. Native to western Asia but long grown all around the Mediterranean, fenugreek is commonly used in the spice blends of India, but in the West it has traditionally been used mostly in medicines.

Fish sauce: Fish sauce is an essential ingredient in the cuisines of Southeast Asia. Known as *nuoc mam* in Vietnam, *nam pla* in Thailand, and *nam pa* in Laos, this thin, brownish sauce is made by packing anchovies or other small fish in salt, allowing them to ferment for three months or more, and then drawing off the accumulated liquid. It may not sound appetizing, but we recommend that you try it because we think you'll be surprised. When used properly, fish sauce works much like salt in Western cooking, adding real depth of flavor without standing out as an individual taste. Keep in mind, too, that its taste is far less pronounced than its aroma.

Galangal: This spice is often thought of as an East Asian version of ginger. The comparison does have some validity, since galangal is a root spice with rhizomes (knobs) that bear a close resemblance to ginger rhizomes. However, galangal is slightly thinner and more smooth-skinned than its better-known cousin, with a creamy white or yellowish interior and a unique, delicate flavor that has more perfume and less bite than ginger. You can substitute ginger root for galangal if necessary.

Ginger: The underground stem, or rhizome, of a perennial tropical plant, ginger is the personification of pungency. It originated in Southeast Asia but is now cultivated throughout the tropics. Best known for its sweet, sharp, aromatic quality, ginger root is used today in cuisines around the world, either fresh or cured, dried, and powdered.

Horseradish (fresh): Although you might never know it if all you've eaten is prepared horseradish, this pungent spice is actually a large root. It is pretty widely available in supermarkets these days, and we really like the mustardy bite of the freshly grated white flesh, which also has a kind of underlying sweetness. When buying horseradish, choose a root that is firm rather than withered and that has no blemishes. Then just peel off the outer skin and grate away.

Jalapeño: The jalapeño deserves special mention as the best-known and most widely consumed fresh chile pepper in the United States. This pepper is plump and bullet-shaped, with a sleek and shiny exterior, about 1 to 1 1/2 inches long. It comes in both red and green varieties and, although relatively low on the heat scale of chile peppers, it still packs a decent punch.

Jicama: This bulbous root vegetable has thin brown skin, a wonderful crisp, crunchy texture, and a sweetish taste that lies somewhere between an apple and a potato. It is widely used in the cooking of Mexico, Latin America, and throughout the Pacific Rim. In the United States, the jicama has become increasingly familiar over the past few years as Latin and Asian ethnic cuisines have gained in popularity, and it can be found in many urban supermarkets.

Juniper berries: Nothing mysterious here; these are the berries of the juniper bush. They are best known as the primary flavoring agent in gin, but in dried form they are also used to flavor meats, sauces, and other dishes. We also like to use the fresh version (well washed, of course) in certain pickles.

Kaffir lime leaves: These are the leaves of a small, pear-shaped, bumpy-skinned lime that grows in Southeast Asia and Hawaii. The fresh leaves, which can often be found in Asian markets, are a bright glossy green and rather oddly shaped, like two leaves attached end to end. They have a wonderful bright citrus flavor with intense floral overtones. Dried lime leaves are also fine but somewhat less aromatic.

Korean red pepper powder: Somewhat similar to cayenne, this powder is made by grinding the husks of dried, seeded chile peppers. It is often used in kimchee because it gives the pickle a nice brick-red color and also distributes the heat evenly throughout.

Lemongrass: Grown throughout tropical Asia, lemongrass provides a fresh, lemony, extremely aromatic flavor that is essential to the cuisines of Thailand and Vietnam. Lemongrass stalks have bulbs at the base like scallions, topped by long, thin, gray-green upper leaves. Stalks can be used whole in liquids from which they are going to be removed before consumption, but only the inner core of the bottom third is tender enough to eat. To prepare lemongrass that you are going to eat, remove the stems above the bottom third (the bulb), and reserve them for use in broths, soups, or teas. Remove the outer leaves from the bottom third of the stalk, and inside you will find a tender core. Mince this core very fine, as you would ginger or garlic, and add as directed. Lemongrass can be found in Asian markets and is increasingly available in supermarkets.

It's Colorless, but Is It Tasteless?

We know that in talking about the water that goes into your pickles we run the risk of seeming overly fussy. But in some recipes water is one of the primary ingredients. Logically enough, that means that if the water has a funny flavor, so will your pickles. If the tap water in your area is highly chlorinated or has "off" tastes, it makes sense to use bottled water in your pickles. There's no need to use a high-end or designer-label water, though; those large plastic jugs of spring water will do the trick just fine.

Mirin: A wine made from fermented rice, mirin is sweet, golden in color, and low in alcohol content. It is used almost exclusively for cooking, adding sweetness and a subtle note of alcohol to a wide variety of dishes. If you can't locate it, you can substitute grape juice, dry sherry, or sweet vermouth.

Mustard seed: Mustard seed, one of the world's oldest spices, comes in three varieties—black, brown, and yellow. The yellow variety, which is actually a kind of off-white, is the least flavorful of the three and the most common in American and European cooking. Black mustard seed has a stronger, deeper flavor, and is more commonly used in Asian and Indian cuisines. The brown variety, often used interchangeably with the black seeds, actually has a bit more bite. We like the black seeds best, but you can always substitute yellow or brown if they are more readily available.

Napa cabbage: See *Chinese cabbage.*

Pickling cucumbers: As their name suggests, these small cucumbers, rather than their larger bretheren, are the ones you should choose for making pickles. There are a number of different individual varieties, but all are picked when they are small and are characterized by thin skins and small seeds, both of which are useful traits when pickling.

Red pepper threads: This Korean chile incarnation consists of seeded, dried red chile peppers that have been cut into extremely thin strips about 2 to 3 inches long, so they literally look like threads. Like all chile products, they do provide some heat, but they are largely decorative. You can substitute ground cayenne pepper for these threads if you are not concerned with aesthetics.

Rice flour: Widely used throughout Asia, this is simply flour made from finely milled long-grain rice. It is used as a thickener in some types of Asian pickles.

Sesame oil: Popular in Asian cooking, this oil comes in two varieties. We prefer the roasted oil, which is quite dark in color and has a pronounced, nutty, almost burned flavor. It is usually used in combination with other, less flavorful oils. You can also get a lighter, blander version, but what's the point?

Sichuan peppercorns: Although they look very much like peppercorns (hence the name), these small red-black dried berries are not a member of the pepper family. Instead, they come from a Chinese ash tree known as fagara. Mildly hot, with a distinctively aromatic flavor, they are used in much the same way as peppercorns in cooking. Like their namesake, they are best ground just before use, since their volatile oils dissipate after they are ground.

Soy sauce: A bedrock ingredient in cuisines all over Asia, soy sauce is one of the world's great fermented products. Simply put, it is made by fermenting boiled soybeans along with a roasted grain, usually wheat, plus water and salt. The resulting sauce has a range of subtle, very complex flavors that belie the simplicity of its ingredients. There are several types of soy sauce, but for pickling we prefer what is known as "light" sauce. This does not mean that it is lighter in calories, but rather lighter in color and flavor. It is also a bit thinner than the darker versions.

Sweet rice flour: This flour, made from finely milled gluti-nous (short-grain) rice, is particularly effective as a thick-ener and is frequently used in sweets.

Star anise: This star-shaped spice is the dried seed pod of an evergreen tree that grows in China and northern Vietnam. With its deep licorice flavor and its eight-pointed, star-shaped pods, it is one of the more exotic spices read-ily available to American cooks. Star anise is both stronger and slightly harsher than anise seed, a spice with which it is often confused although the two are not related.

Turmeric: Turmeric is the dried, powdered underground stem of the turmeric plant, which is grown in tropical cli-mates throughout the world. A primary ingredient of Indian curries, it is also used in mustard and in many of the pickles most familiar to Americans, such as bread-and-butter pickles. When tasted by itself, its flavor is strongly medicinal, bitter, slightly metallic, and earthy. When used in small quantities in cooking, it adds a pleasant, but inde-finable edge of flavor.

Fresh Vegetable Pickles

Your Classic Bread-and Butter Pickles

Fresh Dill Cucumber Pickles

Famous Back Eddy House Pickles

International Garden Pickles:
   Middle Eastern—Style Garden Pickles
   Italian-Style Garden Pickles
   Sichuan Style Garden Pickles
   American Midwest—Style Garden Pickles
   Indian-Style Garden Pickles

Sherry-Pickled Little Chiles with Homemade
   Raisins

Smoky Pickled Corn Circles with Coriander
   Seeds

Crunchy Orange-Pickled Red Onions with
   Chipotles and Tequila

Sweet and Hot Curried Zucchini Pickles

Asian Pickled Cabbage:
   Japanese-Style Cabbage Pickle
   Thai-Style Cabbage Pickle
   Chinese-Style Cabbage Pickle
   Cambodian Style Cabbage Pickle
   Korean-Style Cabbage Pickle

El Salvadoran Pineapple-Pickled Cabbage

Japanese-Style Soy-Pressed Carrots with
   Scallions and Tangerines

Sweet Pickled Hard Red Tomatoes with
   Ginger and Coriander

Pickled Green Tomatoes with Corn and
   Celery

Red Wine—Pickled Beets with Fresh
   Horseradish and Warm Spices

Pickled Turnips:
   Fuchsia Pickled Turnips
   Citrus-Pickled Turnip Wafers with
      Gin and Juniper Berries
   Pickled Turnips with Fennel and
      Star Anise

Pickled Butternut Squash with Sage and
   Cardamom

Corn, Cucumber, and Chile Pickle

Your Classic Bread-and-Butter Pickles [Yield: About 8 cups]

3 pounds pickling cucumbers (less than 5 inches long)

1 large or 2 medium onions (about 1 pound)

3 tablespoons kosher or other coarse salt

1 teaspoon celery seed

1 teaspoon ground turmeric

1 tablespoon yellow mustard seed

1/4 teaspoon ground cloves or allspice (optional)

3 cups cider vinegar

2 1/2 cups brown sugar

Trim and discard the blossom ends of the cucumbers, then peel the onions and cut both into rounds about 1/4 inch thick. In a nonreactive bowl, toss them with the salt, then cover and refrigerate for 1 to 2 hours. Drain well, rinse, drain again, and then set the cucumbers and onions aside.

In a nonreactive pot, combine all the remaining ingredients and bring to a boil over high heat, stirring once or twice to dissolve the brown sugar. Reduce the heat to low, simmer for 3 minutes, and then pour the liquid over the cucumbers and onions. The cucumbers should be amply covered or slightly afloat.

Allow to cool to room temperature, then cover and refrigerate. These pickles have good flavor as soon as they are cool, but the flavor will deepen if you let them sit for 24 hours. They will keep, covered and refrigerated, for a month or more.

It's always fun to take a standard condiment, one that you have known in its commercial incarnation since childhood, and make your own version. This is the pickle that fills that bill; along with the kosher dill, it is a bedrock American classic. Sweet and just a little spicy, it routinely joins catsup and mustard on picnic tables across the country. Making your own not only provides you with much fresher flavor, but also gives you a chance to see how pre-salting keeps even the thinnest wafer of the wiltiest vegetable crunchy. Also, except for the two-hour pre-salting wait, this recipe offers instant gratification—it takes on fantastic flavor by the time it cools.

As with other cucumber pickles, here we remove the blossom ends of the cucumbers. This is necessary not because that section wouldn't taste good, but because it will sometimes soften a pickle. Only a very thin slice need be removed.

Chris always associates these summer pickles with the extra-large camp picnics presided over by his Grandmother Wetzler, a pickle genius without peer. These pickles are always correct as a sandwich accompaniment, particularly with that perfect grilled burger or hot dog. We also like to chop them up and use them in tuna salad or, best of all, to eat them on the beach with last night's cold grilled chicken. Chips are the appropriate side dish here.

Where Are the Gherkins?

We like gherkins, those miniature pickled cucumbers, quite a lot. We are particularly fond of cornichons, the French version of these little snacks. So why don't we have any recipe for them here? The primary reason is that gherkins, which are a different species from other cucumbers, are very hard to find because they are not grown commercially in this country. If you grow them in your garden, feel free to substitute them in any of the cucumber recipes here.

Blossoms and Wax

The blossom ends of cucumbers may contain the residue of certain enzymes, present in larger amounts in the blossoms themselves, that will cause cucumbers to soften as they sit in brine. To avoid this, we recommend the quick and simple remedy of slicing off a very thin slice of the blossom end of the cuke.

Also, cucumbers that you buy in the store may be waxed. The usual remedy for this is to peel the cucumbers, but when pickling you need to leave the skin on. So if the cukes you're about to buy look very glossy, run your fingernail down the side to see if wax comes off. If it does, look elsewhere.

Bring Out the Best in Seeds and Nuts

To intensify the flavor and aroma of spice seeds, it helps to toast them before use, a process that brings out the volatile oils. Since these seeds have often been sitting around for quite a while, this is a step worth taking.

To toast whole spices such as coriander and cumin seeds, simply place them in a dry sauté pan over medium heat and toast, watching carefully and shaking frequently to avoid burning, until the seeds release just the first tiny wisp of smoke, about two to three minutes. At this point, they will also be quite aromatic. Cool the spices to room temperature, and then grind them or, to add additional texture to the dish, use them whole.

The best tool for grinding spices after toasting them is either a spice grinder or (more readily available) an electric coffee grinder that you reserve for that purpose. However, a mortar and pestle will also do the trick, with a little added effort. In the absence of any of these tools, you can crush spices by grinding them against a cutting board with the bottom of a small sauté pan.

Nuts such as almonds, walnuts, and pine nuts also benefit from a brief toasting. The process is the same, with two differences: it takes a little longer, up to four or five minutes, and, since nuts are generally oilier than seeds and therefore easier to burn, they should be removed from the heat when they are lightly browned and have a strong aroma; don't wait for smoke.

Fresh Dill Cucumber Pickles [Yield: 3 1/2 to 4 quarts]

5 to 6 pounds pickling cucumbers (less than 5 inches long)

1 large red onion, peeled, halved, and then cut into half-moons about 1/2 inch thick

1 whole head of garlic (or more to taste), cloves peeled and minced

Handful of dill heads or fronds

2/3 cup peeled, finely grated fresh horseradish (optional)

3 small chiles (or more to taste), slit up one side (optional)

1/4 cup pickling spices (storebought or homemade; see note)

3 cups red wine vinegar

6 cups water

1/2 cup kosher or other coarse salt

Trim and discard the blossom ends of the cucumbers. To accelerate pickling, halve some or all of the cucumbers lengthwise.

Pack all the ingredients except the vinegar, water, and salt into a nonreactive wide-mouth jar, crock, or bowl, saving the smaller and/or halved cucumbers for the top.

In a nonreactive pot, bring the vinegar, water, and salt to a boil over high heat, stirring once or twice to dissolve the salt. Pour the hot mixture over the cucumbers until they are amply immersed. Allow to cool to room temperature, then cover, refrigerate, and allow to stand for 2 days to absorb the expanding flavors of the brine. These cucumbers will keep, covered and refrigerated, for at least 2 months.

Note: For a simple homemade version of the classic pickling spice mixture, combine 1 tablespoon coriander seed, 1 tablespoon mustard seed, 2 teaspoons celery seed, 2 teaspoons peppercorns, 2 whole cloves, and 4 crumbled bay leaves, and mix well. This mixture will keep for months in a sealed container in a cool, dark place.

You've always loved them in jars; now make them yourself and become a hero. Crisp, crunchy, and easy to make, this pickle provides a very tasty compromise for dill pickle lovers in a hurry. For those occasions when you can stand to wait five days or more for fermentation, check out page 92. The main difference is that in this recipe, all of the pickles' tartness derives from fermented grape juice (the vinegar), while some of the slightly more complex tang of cucumbers cured in brine comes from the fermentation of the cucumbers themselves.

Even if you travel this faster lane, we thought you might still want to decide for yourself about the time/crunch ratio. If your cucumbers are fresh and you expect to eat the batch within a week or two, follow this recipe and do nothing more. For crunchier pickles, immerse the cucumbers for eight hours in a brine composed of 10 cups water and 1/4 cup salt, then drain and rinse them before starting this recipe. This process drains the cucumbers of some of their water. For even more crunch, layer a handful of grape, oak, or sour cherry leaves among the cucumbers as you pickle and store them.

We've made the fresh horseradish optional in this recipe because we know some folks might have trouble finding it, but it is worth seeking out. It is one of those unusual ingredients whose presence is at once dominant and subtle.

Always great as a spear with sandwiches, this particular pickle sees the most action at Chris's house as his wife Marcy's favorite afternoon snack.

Famous Back Eddy House Pickles   [Yield: About 12 cups]

2 pounds pickling cucumbers (less than 5 inches long)

3 tablespoons kosher or other coarse salt

3 tablespoons vegetable oil

5 cloves garlic, peeled and bruised

1 pound carrots, peeled and cut on the diagonal into 1/4-inch slices

1 red bell pepper, cut into 1/2-inch pieces

1 green bell pepper, cut into 1/2-inch pieces

2 medium onions, peeled and thinly sliced (about 2 cups)

4 cups cider vinegar

2 1/4 cups brown sugar

1 teaspoon fennel seed

1 teaspoon ground cloves

2 bay leaves

1 tablespoon yellow mustard seed

2 tablespoons prepared Dijon mustard

2 teaspoons whole allspice berries, cracked (see page 74)

2 teaspoons coriander seed, toasted (see page 36) and cracked

Trim and discard the blossom ends of the cucumbers, then cut the cucumbers into rounds about 1/4 to 3/8 inch thick.

In a medium nonreactive bowl, combine the cucumbers and salt and toss to coat. Cover with ice cubes or crushed ice and let stand in the refrigerator for 1 to 2 hours.

Drain the cucumbers, rinse them well, then drain them again. In a medium sauté pan, combine the oil, garlic, carrots, bell peppers, and onions and cook over medium heat, stirring occasionally to prevent browning, until the carrots "sweat" and soften a bit, 5 to 10 minutes.

Remove from the heat and combine with the cucumbers.

In a nonreactive pan, combine the vinegar, brown sugar, and all the spices. Bring to a boil over medium-high heat, stirring to dissolve the sugar. Continue to boil for 5 minutes to flavor the syrup with the spices. Pour the boiling syrup over the vegetables, allow to cool to room temperature, and then cover and refrigerate.

This pickle will keep, covered and refrigerated, for 1 month.

As soon as diners sit down at the Back Eddy, their server brings them a plate of these pickles. It is amazing how fast they disappear. They will no doubt vanish just as fast at your house, but there's no need to worry: this is a supremely adaptable and generous pickle. You can add more vegetables to the container as the supply dwindles, using the same ones as the original batch or adding different ones. (Lightly sautéed turnip slices, for example, work great.) You can also freshen and expand the syrup as needed. To do so, simply combine vinegar and brown sugar in the same proportions as the recipe, bring them to a boil, add spices in the same proportions, and simmer for five minutes. When the syrup is cool, add it to the container.

These pickles are fantastic as low-fat, high-flavor, crunch-imbued appetizers, so serve your guests a plate of them instead of the standard cheese and crackers.

International Garden Pickles

Around the world, one of the most typical "folk" pickles—the pickles that routinely appear on the tables of regular people—is a simple collection of whatever vegetables happen to be ready in the garden at about the same time. We like to use this common denominator of the pickle world to play around with the flavor footprints of various cuisines. With a slight variation in spicing, the inclusion or exclusion of hot peppers, or a drizzle of sesame or soy oil, the same basic ingredients can go from Japanese to Indian to Italian, Middle Eastern, or even Middle American.

We suggest that you use this mini-collection of five recipes as a kind of pickle playground. Mix and match the amounts and types of vegetables you use. Take a big pile of vegetables from the garden and transform them into three or four different flavors of pickles, in any combination that strikes your fancy. Feel free to substitute vegetables that you happen to have in your garden or pick up at the farm stand or produce market. Just try to cut them all into pieces that are more or less the same size, so that the pickling liquid will penetrate them at about the same rate.

Middle Eastern—Style Garden Pickles [Yield: About 8 cups]

8 cups, total, of the following vegetables, in any proportion you want:

carrots, peeled and cut lengthwise into strips 3 to 4 inches long;

green bell peppers, seeded and cut lengthwise into strips;

green beans, whole or halved;

radishes, halved;

cauliflower florets, cut lengthwise into 2 or 3 slices;

green cabbage, outer leaves removed, cut into bite-sized pieces;

red cabbage, cut into bite-sized pieces

5 or 6 large cloves garlic, peeled and crushed

Red pepper flakes or cayenne pepper

2 cups white or red wine vinegar

2 1/3 cups water

1 tablespoon kosher or other coarse salt

In a large nonreactive bowl or jar, combine the vegetables, garlic, and red pepper flakes to taste, and mix well.

In a large nonreactive pitcher or bowl, combine the vinegar, water, and salt, stirring to dissolve the salt. Pour this mixture over the vegetables, mix gently but well, and cover the container with a cloth or napkin. Allow to stand at room temperature for 3 days, then cover and refrigerate.

These pickles can be eaten right away, but their flavor steadily improves over several days. They will keep, covered and refrigerated, for at least 1 month.

Some experts believe that vinegar pickles originated in the Middle East. Whether that is true or not, there is no doubt that cooks from that region favor sour flavors, vinegar and lemon juice among them. If you've ever been to Istanbul and visited a pickle store (yes, they really do have stores there devoted solely to pickles), as Doc did on a recent trip, you would know what we mean. We've lightened this recipe up a bit for American palates, but the flavors of the Middle East still come through.

Picklers of the Middle East also seem to love the pinks and purples that ooze out of slices of beet and red cabbage, so we include some of the latter to color the brine. Use it sparsely for a lighter color or generously as a complete substitute for the green cabbage if you want a darker purple hue.

These pickles are excellent as part of the spread of little dishes known in the Middle East as *mezze*. Try setting them out along with a few cheeses, several kinds of olives, fresh salted tomato wedges, cucumber slices, maybe a dip or two, and some arrack or whiskey to wash it all down with. They are also great with grilled lamb or chicken, and the brine is a wonderful poaching liquid for chicken.

Italian-Style Garden Pickles [Yield: 8 cups]

8 cups, total, of the following vegetables in any proportion you want:

carrots, peeled and cut lengthwise into 3- to 4-inch strips;

red bell peppers, seeded and cut lengthwise into strips;

chile peppers, halved;

green beans, whole or halved;

radishes, stemmed and quartered;

celery (with attached leaves), cut into 2-inch segments;

cauliflower florets, cut lengthwise into 2 or 3 slices

6 or 7 large cloves garlic, peeled and crushed

3 tablespoons, total, of any combination of fresh oregano, fresh thyme, or fresh rosemary

3 cups white wine vinegar

1 3/4 cups water

2 tablespoons sugar

1 tablespoon kosher or other coarse salt

4 bay leaves, crumbled

2 teaspoons fennel seed

2 teaspoons black peppercorns

In a large nonreactive bowl or jar, combine the vegetables with the garlic and fresh herbs and mix well.

In a medium nonreactive saucepan, combine the remaining ingredients and bring to a boil over medium-high heat. Reduce the heat to low and simmer for 3 minutes, stirring once or twice to dissolve the sugar. Immediately pour this hot liquid over the vegetables and mix gently. Allow to cool to room temperature, uncovered, then cover and refrigerate. This pickle is edible within a few hours of cooling, but the flavor improves a lot over the first few days.

These pickles will keep, covered and refrigerated, for at least a month.

This is probably the garden pickle that most of us know best. That's because long-pickled garden vegetables are a standard item on antipasto trays in many Italian restaurants in this country. Unfortunately, many of those restaurants use substandard, commercial versions of this homespun pickle, so the only flavor you get is a rather harsh vinegar. Don't let those experiences deter you from making this pickle. It's easy, it has great flavors, and it looks very pretty in its glass jar or laid out on a platter.

Although we recommend that you refrigerate these pickles just to be sure, they really are fine sitting out at room temperature for the first couple of weeks, just as long as they are covered.

These make excellent pickles for antipasto or appetizer platters, or just to set out in a bowl with any meal.

Sichuan-Style Garden Pickles [Yield: About 6 cups]

10 cups, total, of the following vegetables in any proportion you want:

green cabbage, outer leaves removed, cut into bite-sized pieces;

carrots, peeled and cut lengthwise into strips 3 to 4 inches long;

green beans, whole or halved;

daikon, julienned;

cauliflower florets, cut lengthwise into 2 or 3 slices;

red bell peppers, seeded and cut lengthwise into strips

2 tablespoons plus 1 teaspoon kosher or other coarse salt

2 tablespoons Sichuan peppercorns, toasted (see page 36), or substitute white peppercorns

1 cup rice wine vinegar

2 cups water

1 tablespoon sugar

3-inch piece of fresh ginger as thick as your thumb, peeled and cut into thin disks

Soy sauce, Asian sesame oil, and/or toasted sesame seeds for garnish

In a large nonreactive bowl, combine the vegetables with 2 tablespoons of the salt and mix well. Place a plate on top of the vegetables and weigh it down with a stone, a brick, a large can of vegetables, or any other small, heavy object you have handy. Allow to stand for 1 1/2 to 2 hours, then rinse well, drain, squeeze out the liquid, and drain again.

In a medium nonreactive saucepan, combine the peppercorns, vinegar, water, sugar, ginger, and the remaining 1 teaspoon salt and bring to a boil over medium-high heat. Reduce the heat to low and simmer for 5 minutes, stirring occasionally to dissolve the sugar. Remove from the heat, allow to cool almost to room temperature, and then pour over the vegetables. Allow to stand, covered with a clean cloth or napkin, for 3 to 4 days, then cover tightly and refrigerate.

These vegetable pickles can be eaten 1 day after pickling, but the flavor improves over a few days. Serve them with an optional dash of soy sauce and sesame oil and/or a sprinkle of toasted sesame seeds.

These pickles will keep, covered and refrigerated, for up to 3 weeks.

This takeoff on the standard Chinese "folk" garden pickle does not contain the garlic found in its cousins in other parts of the world. It also benefits from what we like to call "crunch enhancement"—a preliminary salting, rinsing, and squeezing to drain water from the vegetables. The process reduces the volume of the vegetables by about one fourth due to the loss of liquid.

We find this pickle a good candidate for the recharging process. As with soups and stews, the flavors improve as new generations of vegetables are pickled in the ever mellowing and regularly recharged brine. To recharge when you have eaten all the pickles, simply strain the brine, bring it to a simmer on the stove, add the flavorings, allow to cool to room temperature, and add new vegetables. The trick here is to eat the older pickles at the top of the jar so that the replenishments keep getting pushed to the bottom.

This rather light, mild pickle is great as a quick, somewhat unusual, flavor-packed alternative to a traditional salad. Some of our Chinese friends also like to drain these pickles, quickly wok-fry them, and eat them with an extra dash of sesame oil as a wild side dish.

American Midwest—Style Garden Pickles [Yield: 8 cups]

8 cups, total, of the following vegetables, in any proportion you want:

corn circles (sliced corn on the cob) about 1/2 inch thick;

green bell peppers, seeded and cut lengthwise into strips;

green beans, whole or halved;

radishes, stemmed and halved;

green cabbage, outer leaves removed, cut into bite-sized pieces;

cauliflower florets, cut lengthwise into 2 or 3 pieces;

broccoli florets, cut lengthwise into 2 or 3 pieces

3 cloves garlic, peeled and crushed

1 or 2 dried chiles of your choice, whole or crushed (optional)

1 teaspoon celery seed

1 teaspoon ground turmeric

1 tablespoon yellow mustard seed

1/2 teaspoon ground cloves

1/2 teaspoon whole allspice berries

3 cups distilled white vinegar

1 cup white grape juice

3/4 cup sugar

1 tablespoon kosher or other coarse salt

In a large nonreactive jar or bowl, combine all the vegetables but the corn with the garlic and dried chiles, mix well, and set aside.

In a nonreactive saucepan, combine the corn and all the remaining ingredients and bring to a boil over medium-high heat. Reduce the heat to low and simmer for 3 minutes, stirring once or twice to dissolve the sugar and salt. Remove from the heat and immediately pour over the vegetables. Allow to cool to room temperature, uncovered, then cover and refrigerate.

These homey pickles will keep, covered and refrigerated, for about 3 weeks.

This pickle is a tribute to Doc's Grandmother Schwyhart, an Iowa farm woman who was a pickler of awesome talent. To give it a Midwest twinge, we have added some corn circles to the mix. (You nibble off the kernels, leaving the cob behind.) Like many American pickles, this one is a little sweeter than those from other countries.

These pickles are a very good all-purpose condiment. Put them out on a relish plate, serve them as a mid-afternoon snack, add them to a bean salad, chop them up and use them as a relish on top of barbecued chicken . . . the possibilities are virtually endless.

Indian-Style Garden Pickles [Yield: About 7 cups]

1/4 cup vegetable oil

8 cloves garlic, peeled and roughly chopped (about 3 tablespoons)

1/3 cup peeled, grated fresh ginger

1 tablespoon cumin seed

1 tablespoon black mustard seed (cracked with a skillet bottom or slightly ground in a spice or coffee grinder)

2 tablespoons prepared curry powder

1 teaspoon cayenne pepper, or to taste

8 cups, total, of the following vegetables, in any proportion you want:
green cabbage, outer leaves removed, cut into bite-sized pieces;
tart green apple, cored and cut into 8 wedges;
broccoli florets, cut lengthwise into 2 or 3 pieces;

carrots, peeled and cut lengthwise into strips 3 to 4 inches long;
green beans, whole or halved;
cauliflower florets, cut lengthwise into 2 or 3 pieces;
red bell peppers, seeded and cut lengthwise into strips;
small chile peppers, halved

1 tablespoon prepared mustard

1 1/2 cups cider vinegar

1 cup apple juice

1/2 cup water

1/4 cup brown sugar

2 teaspoons kosher or other coarse salt

In a large nonreactive sauté pan, heat the oil over medium-high heat until hot but not smoking. Add the garlic, ginger, cumin, mustard seed, curry powder, and cayenne pepper and sauté, stirring constantly, for 1 minute. (Be careful that the garlic does not brown.) Add the vegetables and continue to sauté, stirring occasionally, until the carrots are crisp-tender and the beans are bright green, about 4 minutes.

Stir in the prepared mustard, mix well, then add the vinegar, apple juice, water, brown sugar, and salt and stir to incorporate. Remove the mixture from the heat and transfer it to a nonreactive bowl or jar. Allow to cool to room temperature, uncovered, then cover and refrigerate.

These pickles are ready for eating within an hour of cooling, but the flavors improve steadily over a few days. They will keep, covered and refrigerated, for at least 3 weeks.

To our minds the most accomplished spice cooks in the world are from India, and that goes for their pickles, too. Typically, pickles from this vast country are quite peppery and are immersed in less liquid than pickles from other regions. There is, for example, a significant tradition of salting and spicing vegetables and placing them in the sunshine with little or no liquid; the liquid that oozes from the vegetables as they interact with the salt provides the pickles' wetness. The sunshine plays a key role in retarding bacterial growth, so we call them "sunshine pickles."

To mimic the flavor of Indian pickles with less time investment, here we sauté some classic Indian pickle spices in hot oil and then add and partially cook the vegetables. Basically, we're making a kind of vegetable curry. We then douse this with some vinegar diluted and sweetened with apple juice and brown sugar. The result is a pickle with a panoply of big flavors that will definitely remind you of India.

These pickles are fantastic with spicy food of any kind, with grilled chicken, or as a way of giving plain rice or pilaf a big flavor boost.

Sherry-Pickled Little Chiles with Homemade Raisins [Yield: 4 cups]

1 1/2 cups seedless white grapes, halved (or substitute 3/4 cup golden raisins)

2 tablespoons sunflower or vegetable oil, plus more for coating grapes

3 cups of your favorite small chiles, slit up one side or punctured twice (or substitute 3 cups peeled white pearl onions)

1 cup shallots, peeled and divided into cloves

1 large clove garlic, peeled and crushed

Piece of fresh ginger the size of your little finger, peeled and julienned

1 tablespoon coriander seed, crushed

2 teaspoons kosher or other coarse salt

2 teaspoons black peppercorns, crushed

1/2 cup dry sherry

1/2 lime, cut into thin wedges

1/2 cup cider vinegar

1/4 cup balsamic vinegar

1 tablespoon Worcestershire sauce

2 tablespoons brown sugar

Preheat the oven or toaster oven to 200°F.

Rub the grape halves lightly with vegetable oil and put them on a baking sheet. Place on the middle rack of the oven and let them dry until they look like plump raisins, about 3 to 4 hours.

In a medium sauté pan over medium-high heat, heat the oil until hot but not smoking. Add the chiles, shallots, garlic, ginger, coriander, salt, and black peppercorns and sauté, shaking frequently to prevent burning, until the chiles are crisp-tender but not browned, 3 to 4 minutes. Add the sherry and simmer for about 1 minute, scraping the bottom

of the pan to incorporate any browned bits into the mixture. Transfer to a medium nonreactive bowl, add the raisins and lime wedges, and stir to combine.

In a small nonreactive saucepan, combine the vinegars, Worcestershire sauce, and brown sugar and bring to a boil over high heat, stirring a few times to dissolve the sugar. Pour this liquid over the chile mixture, allow to cool to room temperature, then cover and refrigerate or store in a cool, dark place.

These pickles will keep well for about a month, covered and stored in a cool, dark place, or for 2 months in the refrigerator.

Chris ran into the combination of chiles and sherry in Bermuda, and really loved it. Here we add some homemade raisins, shallots, and a host of spices to create a souped-up pickle that will wow any chile-head.

This recipe offers the fun of making your own fresh, plump raisins, which will be a revelation if you've only had the rather dry commercial version. If you don't feel like taking up that option, storebought raisins will rise to the occasion quite well, swelling up with pickle juice in an hour or two.

The brine used in this pickle is a high-powered cousin of Worcestershire sauce, which means it makes a fantastic steak sauce; drizzle a little bit over your next grilled steak and you'll see what we mean. The pickled chiles themselves are a great go-along with any red meat.

Smoky Pickled Corn Circles with Coriander Seeds [Yield: About 4 quarts]

2 teaspoons vegetable oil

8 cloves garlic, peeled and crushed

1/2 pound red, orange, and yellow bell peppers, cut into thin rings and seeded

2 large onions, peeled and cut into thin rings

6 tomatillos, papery skins removed, halved (or substitute small green tomatoes, quartered)

4 teaspoons prepared Dijon mustard mixed with 2 teaspoons water

4 cups white wine vinegar

1 cup pineapple juice

2 cups water

1 1/2 cups sugar

2 tablespoons kosher or other coarse salt

2 to 3 tablespoons cilantro berries, crushed (or substitute coriander seed)

1 tablespoon whole cloves

4 to 6 dried chipotle peppers (or substitute 3 to 5 fresh chiles of your choice)

6 ears corn, husked, silked, and cut into rounds about 1/2 to 3/4 inch thick

In a large skillet, heat the oil over medium-high heat until hot but not smoking. Add the garlic, bell peppers, onions, and tomatillos, reduce the heat, and cook, stirring occasionally, until the vegetables "sweat" and are slightly softened and the peppers have brightened in color, about 5 minutes. Be careful not to overcook or brown; they should be crisp-tender. Remove from the heat and set aside.

In a nonreactive pot, combine all the remaining ingredients except the corn and bring to a boil over high heat.

Add the corn rounds; there should be just enough liquid to cover them. Bring back to a boil, reduce the heat to low, and simmer for 5 minutes. Add the reserved vegetables and bring back to a simmer. Turn off the heat and allow to cool to room temperature, uncovered.

Cover and refrigerate. The pickled corn rounds start tasting good by the time they've cooled and will last for 2 weeks, covered and refrigerated. We like them best served chilled.

This chunky way of pickling corn appeals to the fingers as much as to the eye and palate. Chris serves these pickles throughout the late summer at both the Back Eddy and the East Coast Grill and, based on his experience there, you can expect people to suck their cobs for any pickle juice not inhaled with the kernels.

We all love the combination of chipotles and corn, one of those culinary marriages that has been going on for centuries and still feels right. If you're a big fan of heat, though, feel free to increase it here by adding jalapeños, chili powder, red pepper flakes, cayenne pepper, or any bottled hot stuff you have on hand. Cilantro berries, by the way, can be found on cilantro plants that are going to seed. They are small green berries with a taste that is quite different from their dried counterpart, known as coriander seeds. If you don't have any mature cilantro plants around, cracked coriander seeds are a fine substitute.

Set these rounds out as an appetizer with corn bread or as part of an antipasto, or serve them next to grilled pork or as a garnish with sandwiches. When all the cobs are gone, save the liquid to use in a salad dressing, as a fish marinade, or even as a poaching liquid for dark-fleshed fish.

Crunchy Orange-Pickled Red Onions with Chipotles and Tequila   [Yield: About 2 cups]

2 tablespoons kosher or other coarse salt

2 large or 3 medium red onions (about 1 1/2 pounds total), peeled and sliced into disks about 1/2 inch thick

1 Granny Smith apple, cored but not peeled, diced into bite-sized pieces

1 to 2 tablespoons canned chipotle peppers en adobo, depending on your taste for heat

2 large cloves garlic, peeled and minced

1/2 cup distilled white vinegar

1 tablespoon balsamic vinegar

1 tablespoon cumin seed (or substitute 1/2 teaspoon ground cumin)

2 teaspoons coriander seed (or substitute 1 teaspoon ground coriander)

1 tablespoon molasses

Grated zest of 1 orange

3/4 cup orange juice

1/4 cup tequila (or substitute vodka)

Salt and freshly cracked black pepper

In a nonreactive bowl, combine the salt and onion disks and set aside for 1 hour. Drain, rinse well, and drain again. Add the apple, mix gently to combine, and set aside.

Meanwhile, put the chipotles, garlic, vinegars, cumin, coriander, and molasses in a blender or food processor and purée well. Add the orange zest and juice and the tequila and blend for a second more. Add to the apple-onion mixture, mix well, season to taste with salt and pepper, and then cover and refrigerate. Allow to stand overnight before using.

These pickles will keep, covered and refrigerated, indefinitely.

This pickle features one of our favorite flavor combinations, orange juice and smoky chipotle chile peppers, which are basically dried and smoked jalapeños. It also has great texture; with some of their liquid drawn out by salt, the onion slices become as crunchy as a fresh apple. That's why we suggest that they be sliced thickly and their disks be kept more or less intact—so you can really sink your teeth into them.

The pickling liquid is particularly nice here. Just a little dash of it provides a real wake-up call to a standard fruit salad, and it also makes a great marinade for oily fish such as tuna, mackerel, or bluefish. Or try reducing the liquid in a saucepan until it is just sticky, and then painting it onto a pork roast.

This vivid collection of strong Latin flavors is excellent with all grilled foods, but we especially recommend it with steaks and pork chops.

Sweet and Hot Curried Zucchini Pickles [Yield: 8 cups]

3 pounds zucchini, ends trimmed, cut into very thin rounds about 1/8 inch thick

2 red onions about the size of base-balls, peeled and cut into thin slices

3 to 4 colorful chiles of your choice, cut into thin rounds

1/4 cup kosher or other coarse salt

1 cup seedless red and/or green grapes, halved (or substitute golden raisins)

2 3/4 cups distilled white vinegar

3/4 cup sherry

1 1/2 cups orange juice

2 cups sugar

2 tablespoons prepared curry powder

1 1/2 teaspoons cayenne pepper

1 teaspoon whole allspice berries

1 teaspoon whole cloves

3 cloves garlic, peeled and crushed

Piece of fresh ginger the size of your thumb, peeled and cut into thin disks

In a large nonreactive bowl, combine the zucchini, onions, chiles, and salt, and let stand for 1 hour. Drain and rinse twice to remove the salt, then add the grapes and set aside.

In a medium nonreactive saucepan, bring all the remaining ingredients except the ginger to a boil over high heat. Reduce the heat to low and simmer for 3 minutes, stirring once or twice to dissolve the sugar. Pour the hot liquid over the squash mixture; the squash should be amply covered or slightly afloat.

Place the ginger slices inside a fold of plastic wrap and crush with a mallet or other blunt instrument. Add to the squash mixture, allow to cool to room temperature, then cover and refrigerate.

These pickles develop great flavor after a couple of hours of refrigeration and will keep well, covered and refrigerated, for 3 to 4 weeks.

With bright green outer rings set against curry-colored middles and a confetti of sliced chiles, this handsome pickle is a sly trick for transforming the overabundance of squash that backyard gardeners face every summer from burden to bounty. Summer squash is also excellent in this recipe, although the coloring of the final product is not quite as distinctive. If you're one of those ambitious gardeners who plant both types of squash, try combining them in this pickle.

The mild flavor of the squash, when combined with spicy curry and sweet grapes, creates a distinctive Near East flavor that makes a perfect partner for any type of roast or grilled meat, particularly lamb. In addition, the pickling liquid itself makes an excellent vinaigrette or marinade. One lazy afternoon Dan even found that, when used as a base for sautéing, this pickle juice can transform whatever you happen to have on hand—in his particular case a bit of leftover lamb, some eggplant, an onion, and half an apple—into a feast with bold, exciting flavors.

Asian Pickled Cabbage

Cabbage is among the most widely used vegetables in the world. The reasons for this are clear: it grows very easily, it is usually very cheap, and it adapts itself to many culinary uses. But it is in Asia that this humble member of the vast Brassica family reaches its true glory. There are literally hundreds of varieties of Asian cabbages, and they are used in many imaginative ways. This is particularly true of cabbage pickles. Even leaving aside the Korean tradition of kimchee (see page 94), the range of pickled cabbages found throughout Asia is astounding. As with garden pickles (page 40), we think it's fun to play around with flavorings, making the same vegetable into pickles that reflect a range of national flavor footprints. So here are versions that roughly illustrate the similarities and differences in the approach to pickles in Japan, Cambodia, Thailand, China, and Korea.

Japanese-Style Cabbage Pickle [Yield: About 4 cups]

1 large head napa or other Chinese cabbage (about 2 pounds)

Piece of kombu or other seaweed about 4 inches long, cut into thin 2-inch-long strips (optional)

2 scallions (green and white parts), roots trimmed, cut into thin slices on the diagonal

2 tablespoons kosher or other coarse salt

1 lemon, one half zested in thin strips and then juiced, the other half cut into thin slices

1 1/4 cups rice vinegar (or substitute distilled white vinegar)

4 teaspoons light soy sauce

1 cup sake

1 tablespoon sugar

1 teaspoon red pepper flakes or a dash of your favorite hot sauce (optional)

Peel off the first 2 or 3 layers of cabbage leaves and cut them crosswise into 1/2-inch strips. Cut the remaining head of cabbage in half lengthwise, then cut the halves lengthwise through the core to form wedges as thin as possible, making sure each has a bit of the core.

In a large nonreactive bowl, combine the cabbage, kombu, and scallions with the salt. Place a weighted plate on top of the cabbage and allow to stand at room temperature for about 1 hour. Rinse, drain, and squeeze out any additional liquid from the vegetables, then drain well again. Return the cabbage mixture to the bowl, add the lemon zest, juice, and slices, mix well, and set aside.

In a small nonreactive saucepan, bring the vinegar, soy sauce, sake, and sugar to a simmer over medium-high heat, stirring to dissolve the sugar. Remove from the heat and pour the hot liquid over the cabbage. Add red pepper flakes or hot sauce to taste. Allow to cool to room temperature, uncovered, then cover and refrigerate for at least 2 hours, or preferably overnight, before eating.

This pickle will keep, covered and refrigerated, for about 2 weeks.

This book is all about quick, so this is a quick, sweet-and-sour vinegar pickle flavored with a good light Japanese soy sauce and sake. Because we like our flavors bolder, we've added the seaweed known as kombu along with hot peppers and a little more vinegar than traditional Japanese flavor subtlety might require.

Of course, you can leave the kombu out of the pickle, but it isn't really as foreign as you might think. Dan found this out on a frigid February day after a trip to the local health food store, where he had paid $4.29 for a 2.1-ounce package of imported Japanese kombu. On the way home, he decided to go see and smell the only thing outdoors with any "give" left to it—the ocean. (The ground, air, and river had been frozen solid for over a month.) He pulled over to stare at the waves, and Jim Robeson, a local acquaintance, pulled up next to him and said, "I know what you're thinking—seaweed." A bit astounded, Dan took the crumpled paper bag Jim offered, then walked with him gingerly across some icy rocks, where Jim pointed down at some seaweed on the edge of the water and said, "Go ahead, take some. I know you like to cook." This weed was called dulse, he said, adding that he had plenty already dried at home, along with more of the local kombu (dried kelp) that was in the paper bag he had given Dan. As it turned out, his kombu was very much like the version from the store, only not quite as thick. It just goes to show that, if you know where to look, "exotic" ingredients can turn out to be pretty close to home after all.

This light, bright pickle is a perfect accompaniment to any Asian meal or grilled or broiled fish of any kind.

Thai-Style Cabbage Pickle [Yield: About 4 cups]

1 medium head napa or other Chinese cabbage (about 1 1/2 pounds), cored and thinly sliced

2 large carrots, peeled and finely shredded

3 tablespoons kosher or other coarse salt

1/4 cup distilled white vinegar

1 tablespoon minced garlic

1 tablespoon minced fresh chile of your choice

3 tablespoons minced lemongrass (see note), or 1 tablespoon fresh lemon juice

1/4 cup sugar

1/4 cup catsup

1 teaspoon freshly cracked white pepper

2 tablespoons peeled, minced fresh ginger

In a large nonreactive bowl, combine the cabbage, carrots, and salt and mix well. Allow to stand at room temperature for 4 hours, then rinse and drain.

Add the remaining ingredients, mix well, cover, and refrigerate. Allow to stand for 3 to 4 days for the flavor to develop. This pickle will keep, covered and refrigerated, for 2 to 3 weeks.

Using Lemongrass

Only the inner core of the bulb of lemongrass is tender enough to use without cooking. So cut off the top two thirds of the stalk (freeze it for later use; it's great for flavoring soups or stocks) and trim the root end of the remaining bulb. Unwrap the tough outer leaves from the bulb (save them with the upper stalk), and mince the tender inner core.

Like many Southeast Asian dishes, this pickle is at once sweet, hot, and sour, so that it hits just about all of your taste buds at the same time in a real flavor explosion. If you can find fresh lemongrass, it will give the dish a gently sour, highly aromatic underpinning. Dried lemongrass is so far from the real thing, though, that fresh lemon juice, which has a blunter sourness, is a better substitute.

The approach we use here is a bit simpler than that used with other Asian-style cabbage pickles, since we use less liquid and simply combine the liquid and solid ingredients without first simmering the liquids. This results in a drier pickle, somewhat more like a salad, which we like with this particular combination of flavors.

This simple pickle is an excellent accompaniment to curries or any other spicy hot dish.

Chinese-Style Cabbage Pickle [Yield: About 5 cups]

1 small head red cabbage (about
  1 1/4 pounds), cored and cut into
  strips about 5 inches long and 1/4
  inch wide

1 red bell pepper, seeded and cut into
  long strips about 1/4 inch wide

3 scallions (green and white parts),
  roots trimmed, cut into thin rounds
  on the diagonal

2 tablespoons kosher or other
  coarse salt

1 tablespoon Asian sesame oil

2 teaspoons vegetable oil

1 teaspoon peeled, finely grated fresh
  ginger

2 tablespoons sesame seed

1/2 cup rice wine vinegar

1 tablespoon sugar

Freshly cracked white pepper
  (or substitute black)

In a large nonreactive bowl, combine the cabbage, bell pepper, and scallions with the salt and toss well to coat. Place a weighted plate on top of the cabbage and allow it to stand at room temperature for 1 to 2 hours. Drain, rinse well, drain again, and gently squeeze any liquid out of the vegetables. Set aside.

In a large sauté pan, combine the sesame and vegetable oils and heat over medium-high heat until hot but not smoking. Add the ginger and sesame seed and sauté, stirring frequently, for 1 minute. Add the reserved vegetables and sauté, stirring constantly, for 2 minutes. Remove from the heat, add the vinegar, sugar, and white pepper to taste, and mix well. Allow to cool to room temperature, then cover and refrigerate.

This pickle will keep, covered and refrigerated, for about 2 weeks.

Like most other nonfermented Chinese pickles, this one is a bit more in the salad direction than its Euro/American/Middle Eastern counterparts, with a lower proportion of liquid to solids. The hour or two with the salt makes the cabbage limp but eternally crunchy; it also shrinks the volume by about half a cup.

We like to use red cabbage with this one for a bit of a change, but you can easily substitute green cabbage.

Napa cabbage would work fine, too, but its gentler texture will result in a somewhat less crisp pickle, although still satisfyingly crunchy.

Serve this pickle as a kind of side salad with fish or pork, or add it to rice for a quick vegetarian lunch.

Cambodian-Style Cabbage Pickle [Yield: About 4 cups]

1 large head napa or other Chinese cabbage (about 2 pounds)

2 tablespoons kosher or other coarse salt

1 small chile of your choice or half a red bell pepper, seeded and cut into thin strips

4 scallions, (green and white parts), roots trimmed, cut into thin slices on the diagonal

3 to 4 tablespoons sugar

1 1/2 cups water

Juice and grated zest of 1 lime

1 1/3 cups distilled white vinegar

1 teaspoon ground turmeric

2 tablespoons peeled, minced galangal (or substitute peeled, minced fresh ginger)

6 kaffir lime leaves (or substitute another tablespoon of lime juice)

4 stalks lemongrass, bottom third only, tough outer layer peeled off and inner core minced

5 cloves garlic, peeled and crushed

Several dashes of your favorite hot sauce

2 teaspoons Southeast Asian fish sauce, or to taste (or substitute 1 teaspoon salt)

Peel off 8 to 10 of the outermost cabbage leaves and cut crosswise into 1/2-inch thick strips, discarding any damaged or discolored sections. Cut the remaining cabbage head in half lengthwise, then cut the halves lengthwise again through the core to form 4 thin wedges.

The idea for this pickle came from a Cambodian grocery in Providence, Rhode Island, where Dan first looked for ingredients to give Cambodian cooking a try. After a few minutes of wandering the aisles in ignorance and awe, he stopped to chat with the woman behind the counter, who was making something in a bowl. It was yellow and smelled good. She asked a few questions, and then said, "I think what you want is this," and held the bowl out under his chin for him to smell. The perfume of this mix got to him. She was dry-grinding it by hand between customers, as she often did, and wrapping it in cellophane for sale in small Styrofoam trays set next to some greens. He bought several packages that day, as well as the turmeric, lemongrass, lime, lime leaves, garlic, and galangal to make his own from scratch.

For about the next six months he was besotted with this stunningly aromatic mixture. He used it on everything: in noodles, salads, and soups, and sprinkled it on shrimp, rice, and beef. Finally he gave some to a Cambodian American named Khemarak who works at the Back Eddy, asking him to bring it home for his mother to check out its flavor. Khemarak returned with a very similar mixture from his mother, who sent a message that, although it's hard to dry-grind, puréeing it in some liquid is simple. So that's what we do here. As you'll see, this magic spice mix can turn even humble cabbage into an incredible taste medley.

Because of his fondness for Southeast Asian flavors, this is one of Doc's favorite pickles. He likes it with grilled steak, grilled vegetables, as a relish with fish, or just as a snack.

In a large nonreactive bowl, combine the cabbage, salt, chile, and scallions and mix well. Place a weighted plate on top of this mixture and allow it to stand at room temperature for about 1 hour. Rinse, drain, and squeeze out any additional liquid from the vegetables. Rinse and dry the bowl, return the drained cabbage to it, and set aside.

In a nonreactive saucepan, combine the sugar, water, lime juice, and vinegar and bring to a simmer over medium-high heat, stirring to dissolve the sugar. Remove from the heat.

In a blender or food processor, combine the lime zest, turmeric, galangal, lime leaves, lemongrass, and garlic, along with 1/2 cup of the warmed liquid, and purée, adding more liquid as needed to make a smooth purée. Add the rest of the liquid, pulse several times to combine, and then pour over the cabbage. Add the hot sauce and fish sauce and toss well to mix. Allow to cool to room temperature, uncovered, then cover and refrigerate.

This pickle will keep, covered and refrigerated, for up to 4 weeks.

Korean-Style Cabbage Pickle [Yield: 4 to 6 cups]

1 small head napa or other Chinese cabbage (about 1 1/4 pounds)

3 tablespoons kosher or other coarse salt

1 medium daikon radish (about 1/2 pound), julienned (1 1/2 to 2 cups)

5 scallions (green and white parts), roots trimmed, split lengthwise and cut crosswise into thirds

1 tablespoon rice flour (or substitute 3 tablespoons wheat flour)

3/4 cup water (1/2 cup water if using wheat flour)

4 teaspoons distilled white vinegar

4 teaspoons fresh lemon juice

4 teaspoons sugar

2 teaspoons salted anchovy paste or salted shrimp paste (or substitute 1/4 cup Southeast Asian fish sauce) (optional)

3 tablespoons Korean dried hot red pepper powder or paste (or substitute dried red pepper flakes)

1 tablespoon peeled, minced fresh ginger

1 1/2 tablespoons minced garlic

This pickle is hot and garlicky, the Korean tradition offering sharp contrast to the subtlety of China and (even more) of Japan. As with quick Chinese cabbage and dill pickles, this is a tasty vinegar and lemon alternative to a "folk" pickle that ordinarily relies on fermentation for its sourness. However, nothing prevents this recipe from taking on some more sourness from fermentation after a little while, except that people are usually in such a hurry to eat it while it's fresh.

The flour, which is somewhat unusual in the world of pickling, actually provides a thicker, pastier vehicle for flavorings that works very well. Traditional recipes call for rice flour, but if you don't have it, just use triple the amount of wheat flour.

You will notice that this recipe has a number of ingredients—daikon radish, rice flour, anchovy paste, Korean hot pepper powder—that you may find unfamiliar. But they are fun to play around with, and they can all be found in most large Asian markets or in Korean or Southeast Asian stores. As with other Asian pickles, feel free to leave out the fish paste if you don't like that flavor.

Try this pickle alongside grilled fish or roast chicken, or as an accompaniment to any Asian dish.

Make shallow cuts in the base of the cabbage. Pry it in half lengthwise with your fingers and then again into quarters. Sprinkle the salt among all the leaves, salting the thicker bottoms more than the delicate tops. Arrange the cabbage quarters at an angle in a colander or bowl and let them sit at room temperature to wilt and drain for about 2 hours, until the leaves are flexible enough to fold in half without breaking. Rinse the cabbage to remove the salt, and squeeze to remove any excess water. Drain well, and cut the cabbage crosswise into bite-sized pieces.

In a nonreactive bowl, combine the cabbage with the radish and scallions and mix well.

In a small nonreactive saucepan, combine the flour, water, vinegar, lemon juice, sugar, anchovy paste, and red pepper powder, and bring to a boil over medium-high heat. Cook for just 1 minute, whisking to blend in the flour and dissolve the sugar. Remove from the heat and add the ginger and garlic. Allow to cool almost to room temperature, then pour over the cabbage and radish, mixing well. Add more salt and/or sugar to taste.

This pickle can be served immediately, but its flavors will improve overnight. It will keep, covered and refrigerated, for 3 to 4 weeks.

El Salvadoran Pineapple-Pickled Cabbage [Yield: About 5 cups]

1 small head green cabbage, cored and
   cut into very thin slices

1 small red onion, peeled, halved,
   and cut into very thin slices

1 medium carrot, peeled and cut into
   very thin circles

1 cup diced fresh pineapple

1 1/2 teaspoons minced garlic

3/4 cup distilled white vinegar

1/4 cup pineapple juice

2 to 4 jalapeños or other fresh chiles
   of your choice, cut into thin slices

Salt and freshly cracked black pepper
   to taste

In a large nonreactive bowl, combine all ingredients and toss to mix well. Allow the mixture to stand, covered and refrigerated, for about 12 hours, stirring occasionally.

This pickle will keep, covered and refrigerated, for about 1 week.

This pickle is based on the classic El Salvadoran dish called *cordito*. It has some innovations, though, specifically some pineapple to counteract the sourness of the vinegar and some jalapeños to pep it up a bit. This version was invented by Amilcar and Elmer, the El Salvadoran day chefs at the East Coast Grill in Cambridge, Massachusetts, who serve it as an accompaniment to the pork *chicharrónes* that they cook for breakfast.

This pickle is *muy bueno* with grilled pork chops or with roasted chicken and a pile of fresh tortillas.

Japanese-Style Soy-Pressed Carrots with Scallions and Tangerines

[Yield: About 3 cups]

1 pound carrots, peeled and cut into thin strips about 3 inches long (about 5 cups)

1/2 cup Japanese light soy sauce

1/3 cup mirin (or substitute white grape juice)

1/4 cup rice vinegar (or substitute distilled white vinegar)

2 tablespoons fresh lime juice

Grated zest of 2 tangerines, clementines, or mandarin oranges

1/2 cup peeled, grated fresh horseradish

3 tangerines, clementines, or mandarin oranges, peeled and sectioned (or substitute one 11-ounce can mandarin orange sections with liquid)

2 scallions (green and white parts), roots trimmed, cut into thin rounds on the diagonal

2 teaspoons black sesame seed, toasted (see page 36)

In a nonreactive crock, jar, or bowl (the more cylindrical and steep-sided the better), combine the carrots, soy, mirin, vinegar, lime juice, zest, and horseradish. Place a weighted plate on top of the carrots and allow to stand for about 24 hours. Add the tangerine sections, scallions, and sesame seed and mix well, then cover and refrigerate.

These pickles are ready to eat after an hour or two, but their flavor will improve after 1 or 2 days. They will keep, covered and refrigerated, for 2 to 3 weeks.

As far as we can tell, the Japanese regularly use the widest variety of pickling techniques of any other country or region on the planet. Pickles are fundamental to the gestalt of Japanese dining, providing little tastes to stimulate the appetite, and there is hardly a vegetable that they don't pickle. We have heard it said, in fact, that pickles are to Japanese cuisine what cheese is to French cuisine, a comparison borne out by the fact that pickles are the most frequent ending to a Japanese meal.

Most Japanese home kitchens include a device called a *shokutaka tsukemono ki*, or pickle press, which is basically a small tub with an inner top that can be screwed down to press the vegetables down into the brining liquid. It can also be used to squeeze liquid out of the vegetables after brining. We mimic that here with the simple apparatus of a weighted plate.

This sugarless pickle gets its sweetness from mirin, a sweet, golden Japanese wine made from fermented rice. If you can't locate mirin, you can substitute white grape juice, but you will lose a little of the flavor undertones. If you substitute canned mandarin orange segments for the tangerines, add the canned syrup for both flavor and sweetness.

This pickle is especially good with a nice piece of grilled oily fish such as tuna, salmon, or bluefish. It's also good straight up with white or brown rice, as an addition to a spinach salad, or alongside roast chicken.

Sweet Pickled Hard Red Tomatoes with Ginger and Coriander [Yield: 4 cups]

2 pounds unripe tomatoes (about 4 the size of baseballs), cut into wedges about 1/8 inch thick (4 to 5 cups)

2 medium red onions, peeled and cut into rounds about 1/2 inch thick (about 1 1/4 cups)

2 tablespoons kosher or other coarse salt

Piece of fresh ginger about the size of your thumb, peeled and cut into thin disks

1 1/2 cups red wine vinegar

3/4 cup sugar

4 teaspoons coriander seed, toasted (see page 36) and ground in a spice mill or coffee grinder

In a medium nonreactive bowl, combine the tomatoes and onions with the salt and toss to mix well. Cover, refrigerate, and allow to stand for at least 4 hours or overnight. Drain and rinse twice to remove the salt, then set aside.

Place the ginger in a fold of plastic wrap to catch the juices, and crush with a mallet or other heavy object.

In a nonreactive saucepan, combine the ginger with the remaining ingredients and bring to a boil over medium-high heat, stirring once or twice to dissolve the sugar. Reduce the heat to low and simmer for 5 minutes, stirring occasionally. Remove from the heat, allow to cool for 5 minutes, then pour over the tomatoes and onions. Allow to cool to room temperature, uncovered, then cover and refrigerate.

These pickles will keep, covered and refrigerated, for 2 weeks.

This recipe, which calls for unripe tomatoes, takes advantage of the fact that these garden favorites actually ripen from the inside out. This means that plump green tomatoes are often already turning pink inside. At this stage, not only are they pretty to look at, but they offer an interesting combination of flavors as well.

Pickling these hard reds and greens offers a way to expand the harvest season on both ends, offering early-summer gratification as well as salvation for immature fruits threatened by frost at season's end. This recipe will also work wonders with the hard, pale versions that abound on winter grocery shelves.

We love these pickles with striped bass or other mild fish. They also make an excellent antipasto number or just a midday snack. Use the pickling juice as a vinaigrette for any lettuce salad, or reduce some of it by boiling it for a minute or two over high heat, and then use it as a glaze for roast beef.

Pickled Green Tomatoes with Corn and Celery [Yield: About 6 cups]

4 green tomatoes about the size of baseballs, cut into thin slices

2 tablespoons kosher or other coarse salt

1 red bell pepper, diced small

2 celery stalks, cut crosswise into pieces about 1/4 inch wide

1 red onion, peeled and diced small

2 cups distilled white vinegar

2 cups sugar

10 whole cloves

1 teaspoon ground cinnamon

Kernels from 3 ears corn

Additional salt and freshly cracked black pepper

Rub the tomato slices with the salt and allow to stand overnight, covered and refrigerated. In the morning, drain the tomato slices, rinse them well, and then squeeze them very gently to remove excess moisture. Place the tomatoes in a large bowl along with the bell pepper, celery, and onion.

In a large saucepan, combine the vinegar, sugar, cloves, and cinnamon, and bring to a boil over high heat, stirring occasionally to dissolve the sugar. Add the corn and simmer for 30 seconds.

Remove from the heat and pour over the tomato mixture. Allow to cool to room temperature, season to taste with salt and pepper, and then cover and refrigerate.

This pickle will keep, covered and refrigerated, for 3 to 4 weeks.

There are times, particularly at the end of the growing season, when you can't wait for tomatoes to come to the state of hard near-ripeness described in the recipe for Sweet Pickled Hard Red Tomatoes with Ginger and Coriander (previous page). You have to either use the tomatoes green or let them go by. This recipe is designed for just those times. Letting the tomatoes sit overnight with salt on them not only draws out some moisture so they stay crisp in the pickling liquid, but paradoxically gives them a slightly more tender texture as well.

This is a fantastic pickle to take along on a picnic.

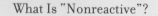

What Is "Nonreactive"?

Throughout the recipes in this book, we tell you to use *nonreactive* bowls, pans, and jar lids. What is this all about? We're simply talking about materials that do not react chemically with acids. Since most pickles rely heavily on acidic liquids such as vinegar and citrus juices, it is particularly important that you use nonreactive cookware. The only metals that you have to worry about, though, are cast iron and aluminum. Stainless steel, enameled cast iron, anodized aluminum, and nonstick surfaces are all fine. What happens if you goof and use aluminum or cast iron? Not that much—the liquid will turn a bit grayish and will taste slightly metallic. Still, it is definitely something you want to avoid.

Red Wine—Pickled Beets with Fresh Horseradish and Warm Spices [Yield: 4 cups]

2 pounds beets (about 5 medium)

1/4 cup grated orange zest (from about 1 1/2 oranges)

1/4 cup orange juice

3/4 cup red wine vinegar

3/4 cup dry red wine

1/2 cup brown sugar

1 teaspoon whole allspice berries

2 teaspoons whole cloves

1/4 cup peeled and coarsely grated fresh horseradish

2 teaspoons kosher or other coarse salt

Freshly cracked black pepper

Cook the beets in boiling salted water until tender, about 25 to 30 minutes. When they are cool enough to handle, peel and cut them into 3/8- to 1/2-inch cubes or disks about 1/4 inch thick, then transfer them to a nonreactive bowl or jar.

In a nonreactive saucepan, bring the remaining ingredients to a boil over high heat. Reduce the heat to low and simmer for 3 minutes, stirring occasionally to dissolve the brown sugar. Pour this liquid over the beets, allow them to cool to room temperature, uncovered, and then cover and refrigerate.

These beets will keep, covered and refrigerated, for 3 to 4 weeks.

As a youth, Doc was a big fan of his grandmother's pickled beets. Not only were they delicious in and of themselves, but their appearance on a relish tray at her house invariably meant that a big-deal dinner was about to follow. These magnificently full-flavored pickles are a worthy successor. The orange zest and warm spices reinforce the sweet, fruity flavor of the beets, while the horseradish matches nicely with the beets' earthy flavor underpinnings. You can use horseradish from a jar here, but it's really worth finding the real thing.

These beets are great as part of an antipasto platter or as a salad ingredient. Chris also likes to chop them up and use them as an interesting partner to roasted or braised meats, particularly pot roast.

Pickled Turnips

Pickled turnips have deep, fermented "roots" in Korea, the Middle East, Eastern Europe, and even Germany. Turnips are an excellent vehicle for tangy pickle flavors and bright colors. We prefer to use Westport's own Macomber turnips, a local hybrid that is actually a cross between a rutabaga and a radish, for their extraordinary sweetness and whiteness. Especially where pickles are concerned, the snowy color of the Macomber acts as the perfect canvas for added hues. Plus they're so sweet that you just can't cut them up for pickles without eating a handful raw in the process. For those of you who are unlucky enough to live far from Westport, try finding a locally grown turnip and experiment with it—its freshness will make it the best turnip you can buy.

Citrus–Pickled Turnip Wafers with Gin and Juniper Berries, Fuschia Pickled Turnips, Pickled Turnips with Fennel and Star Anise

Fuchsia Pickled Turnips [Yield: About 6 cups]

2 cups cranberry juice

1 1/2 cups red or white wine vinegar

1 cup water

1/4 cup kosher or other coarse salt

3 or 4 cloves garlic, peeled and crushed

2-inch piece of fresh horseradish root, peeled and grated (about 1/4 cup), or 1/4 cup prepared horseradish

1 medium beet, peeled, halved, and each half cut into 4 or 5 disks about 1/4 inch thick

2 pounds turnips, preferably white, cut lengthwise into 1-inch-thick wedges

In a medium nonreactive saucepan, combine the cranberry juice, vinegar, water, salt, and garlic and bring to a boil over high heat, stirring once or twice to dissolve the salt.

Meanwhile, toss the horseradish, beet, and turnips together in a large nonreactive bowl and pack into jars if desired. When the liquid comes to a boil, pour it over the turnips and beet until they are well covered. Let the mixture cool to room temperature, then cover and refrigerate.

These already blushing pickles will deepen in color and flavor within 24 hours and will keep, covered and refrigerated, for several months.

As the grandson of Lebanese immigrants, Dan grew up with a simpler version of this flamboyant pickle on the table—one that was salty and more vinegary and lacked the cranberry and horseradish. To him, this vibrantly colored pickle is about fasting, feasting, and whiskey. Fasting because it was often served in vivid contrast to a delicious but drab Lenten dish of brown lentils and caramelized onions. Feasting because its redness evokes holiday color. And whiskey because these pickles are often among the *mezze* (antipasto) snacks of fresh cheese, garden vegetables, brined olives, and sometimes raw lamb that are eaten by Dan's grandfather and his pals, who have been known to wash them down with a shot of whiskey or arrack.

The simpler and more traditional version of this recipe remains the Lebanese national pickle and is also fundamental to the traditions of several neighboring Middle Eastern countries. Out of respect for the pickle's "roots," here the turnips are cut into wedges; but turnips cut into uniform bite-sized pieces between 1/4 and 1/2 inch thick will pickle faster.

Try these pickles as appetizers or serve them as a side dish with prime rib or any other beef roast. Or add a few cloves for holiday flavor and pack the pickles into decorative glass jars, and a good portion of your holiday gift shopping will be done.

Citrus-Pickled Turnip Wafers with Gin and Juniper Berries [Yield: About 6 cups]

2 pounds small turnips (up to 1/2 pound each), peeled and cut into wafers about 1/4 inch thick

3 tablespoons kosher or other coarse salt

Zest of 1 orange, julienned

Zest of 2 lemons, julienned

Zest of 2 limes, julienned

2/3 cup orange juice

1 cup fresh lemon juice

1 cup fresh lime juice

1/4 cup white wine vinegar

1 cup gin

1/2 cup white grape juice

2 tablespoons juniper berries, slightly crushed (optional)

4 teaspoons peeled, finely minced fresh ginger

1/2 teaspoon ground turmeric

In a nonreactive bowl, combine the turnip wafers with the salt and toss well. Set aside for about 1 hour, or until the turnips are limp enough to fold without breaking. Drain and rinse twice to remove the salt.

Place the turnip wafers in a large nonreactive bowl or in glass jars, add all the remaining ingredients, cover, and refrigerate.

The flavors begin to develop almost immediately in this pickle, but they improve significantly overnight as the juniper berries steep in the liquid. These pickles will keep, covered and refrigerated, for 3 to 4 weeks.

These sunny yellow pickles, streaked with long, curly strands of green, yellow, and orange zest, taste as bright as they look. Purplish-blue juniper berries—the source of gin's resinous, piney scent—echo gin-and-lemonade flavors with every bite. The berries grow wild all over Westport, although the tree is not native to North America.

We think that clear alcoholic beverages such as gin and tequila are particularly nice additions to pickles. Maybe it's because, since vinegars are products of double fermentation, these products of single fermentation add a resonant flavor. In any case, this pickle is awesome with seafood of any kind and is also great next to venison, game birds, or roasted poultry.

Pickled Turnips with Fennel and Star Anise [Yield: About 8 cups]

2 pounds turnips, peeled

1 fennel bulb with fronds

1/2 cup pink peppercorns

1 tablespoon kosher or other coarse
salt

1 tablespoon whole allspice berries

1 teaspoon whole cloves

1 tablespoon anise seed

3 bay leaves

1/2 cup whole star anise

1 cup sugar

3 cups white balsamic vinegar (or
substitute white wine vinegar or rice
wine vinegar)

1 1/2 cups white grape juice

Cut each turnip lengthwise into 8 wedges, then cut each wedge crosswise into triangles about 1/4 to 1/2 inch thick.

Tear the feathery fennel fronds from the stalks and set aside. Cut the fennel stalks from the bulb, and slice them crosswise into 1/4-inch-thick disks. Split the fennel bulb lengthwise into 8 or more wedges by making shallow cuts into its base and using your fingers to pry it open along its natural seams.

In a nonreactive bowl or jar, combine the pink peppercorns, turnips, and all the fennel pieces except the fronds. Combine the remaining ingredients except the fronds in a nonreactive saucepan and bring to a boil over medium-high heat. Reduce the heat to low and simmer for 3 minutes, stirring occasionally.

Pour the hot liquid over the vegetables and allow them to cool to room temperature, uncovered. Add the fennel fronds, stir to mix, and then cover and refrigerate.

These pickles take on enough flavor to be eaten with great pleasure after chilling for just a few hours, but they will keep well, covered and refrigerated, for at least 6 weeks.

This gorgeous pickle was conceived by Dan, appropriately enough, as a bridal pickle. It appeared as a star on Chris and Marcy's wedding pickle buffet (that's right, they had a pickle buffet at their reception) and reprised its success at the Back Eddy's Millennium Party on New Year's Eve, 1999.

Turnips and other crunchy roots like carrots, daikon, and jicama, can be sliced into rounds and punched into numbers, letters, stars, bells, or any other shape with cookie cutters. Riffing on that concept, for the Back Eddy's Millennium Party we served these white pickled turnips with pink peppercorns, fennel fronds, and star anise in small bowls, topped with stars punched from turnip rounds, pickled and curried gold.

There's no need to get that fancy, though; these pickles are beautiful and delicious just as they are made here. They're excellent with lamb dishes of any kind or served as an antipasto with a couple of cheeses and a handful of olives.

Pickled Butternut Squash with Sage and Cardamom [Yield: About 4 cups]

3-pound butternut squash, other winter squash, or pumpkin, peeled, seeded, and cut into 3/4-inch cubes (about 5 cups)

1 1/2 tablespoons kosher or other coarse salt

8 whole sage leaves

1 teaspoon cardamom seed (without pods), lightly crushed

2/3 cup brown sugar

1 2/3 cups cider vinegar

3/4 cup apple juice

In a nonreactive bowl, combine the squash and salt, toss to coat, and allow to stand at room temperature for about 4 hours. Drain, rinse well, and squeeze out extra moisture by the handfuls.

In a medium nonreactive pot, combine all the remaining ingredients and bring to a boil over medium-high heat, stirring once or twice to dissolve the brown sugar. Add the squash, bring back just to a simmer, then remove from the heat and allow to cool to room temperature, uncovered.

When the mixture has cooled to room temperature, cover and refrigerate it.

The squash will be tasty in about 2 hours but will improve in flavor if allowed to sit overnight. This pickle will keep, covered and refrigerated, for about 2 months.

It's somewhat unusual to pickle hard squashes like butternut or acorn, but it is actually a very nice way to use them. The pickle is firm and crunchy, and the sage and cardamom are a wonderful duo, aromatic and autumnal.

You can buy cardamom in either pod or seed form. Either will do, but seeds still in the pods tend to retain more of their volatile oils. Each pod contains about 15 or 20 seeds, which you can extract just by crushing the pod in your finger and picking out the seeds.

Serve these with braised meats, stews, or chopped up and mixed with couscous as a side dish.

Crack Them Up

Whole spice berries such as allspice, coriander, and peppercorns will give up their flavors more quickly if they are just slightly cracked. This is a big advantage when making the quick pickles in this book, intended to be eaten over a few days or, at most, weeks. There are several ways to crack spice berries. Many chefs like to use the flat blade of a chef's knife. This is a perfectly acceptable method, especially when you are cracking only a tablespoon or two of berries. Another option, particularly useful for larger quantities, is to use the bottom of a small but heavy sauté pan. Just press down and roll the pan back and forth over the berries once or twice, and the job is done.

Corn, Cucumber, and Chile Pickle [Yield: About 6 cups]

1 medium cucumber, blossom end trimmed, unpeeled, cut into small dice (about 1 cup)

2 teaspoons kosher or other coarse salt

1 3/4 cups distilled white vinegar

1/2 cup pineapple juice

2/3 cup sugar

2 tablespoons peeled, minced fresh ginger

1 tablespoon minced garlic

1 tablespoon mustard seed

1 tablespoon celery seed

9 ears corn, blanched in boiling, salted water for 2 minutes, drained, and the kernels cut off the cobs (about 4 cups of kernels)

1/4 to 3/4 cup finely diced fresh chiles of your choice

3/4 cup diced onion

Juice of 1/2 lime

Salt and freshly cracked white pepper

In a large nonreactive bowl, combine the cucumber and salt, mix well, and allow to stand for 1 hour. Drain and rinse twice to remove the salt, then set aside.

In a nonreactive saucepan, combine the vinegar, pineapple juice, sugar, ginger, garlic, mustard seed, and celery seed and bring to a boil over high heat, stirring once or twice to dissolve the sugar. Add the corn kernels, chiles, and onion and bring back to a boil, then reduce the heat to low and simmer until the corn is just tender, 5 to 7 minutes. Remove from the heat and stir in the lime juice and salt and pepper to taste. Cool the liquid to room temperature, uncovered, then pour over the cucumbers, cover, and refrigerate.

These pickles will keep, covered and refrigerated, for 2 to 3 weeks.

This is the pickle that helped Dan learn an important lesson about the inner nature of pickles in general. He had originally made a much milder version of this recipe, basically flavored only with a little vinegar and cumin. His thought was that this was the best way to preserve the fresh flavor of the first corn crop of the season. But, knowing his co-workers' penchant for strong flavors, he also made a more aggressively flavored version. He didn't really like the stronger one as much, but his co-workers unanimously favored it for its ability to really "set up" the grilled native scallops they were planning to serve it with at the Back Eddy restaurant later that week. When Dan tried it with the scallops the scales fell from his eyes and he realized that in its heart a true pickle wants to pack a real flavor punch.

This pickle (which now packs quite a punch, indeed) bears a close resemblance to the relish known as piccalilli. We love it on sandwiches or with any grilled food; it's also a great way to pick up the flavor of a seafood salad.

Fresh Fruit Pickles

Super-Sweet Clove-Scented
   Watermelon Rind Pickles

Rhubarb Pickles with Caramelized Onions

Pickled Grapes and Jicama with Celery Seed

Balsamic-Pickled Peaches

Balsamic-Pickled Grapefruit with
   Shaved Fennel

Bourbon Pickled Apricots

Classic Pickled Crab Apples

Soy-and-Ginger-Pickled Green Mango

Pickled Pineapple and Cranberries in
   Apple Juice

Super-Sweet Clove-Scented Watermelon Rind Pickles [Yield: About 6 cups]

4 cups white part of watermelon rind (no green, no red), cut into 1/2-inch cubes

1/4 cup kosher or other coarse salt

2 cups sugar

1 cup cider vinegar

10 whole cloves

In a large bowl, combine the rind and the salt and toss to coat. Cover and refrigerate overnight.

Rinse the cubed rind well, drain, and place in a medium saucepan with water to cover. Bring to a boil over high heat, then reduce the heat to low and simmer for 10 minutes. Remove from the heat, drain in a colander, and set aside.

In the same saucepan, combine the sugar, vinegar, and cloves and bring to a boil over high heat. Add the reserved rind, bring to a boil again, reduce the heat to low, and simmer for 10 minutes.

Remove the mixture from the heat and allow to cool to room temperature. Pour into jars, seal tightly, and refrigerate.

Allow these pickles to stand in the refrigerator for 1 week before using. They will keep, covered and refrigerated, for up to 6 weeks.

This was the favorite pickle of Chris's Grandma Wetzler, an acknowledged virtuoso of the pickle jar. Like many other American pickles, it's more sweet than sour, but it still has that underlying sweet-tart dynamic that our taste buds find so enticing. Plus it is very satisfying to make something really tasty out of an ingredient that would otherwise simply be tossed out.

We love these pickles by themselves, with ham, or chopped up and used in egg or tuna salad.

Rhubarb Pickles with Caramelized Onions [Yield: About 4 cups]

1 pound fresh rhubarb, cut into 1-inch chunks

3 tablespoons kosher or other coarse salt

1/4 cup vegetable oil

3 onions, peeled and cut into small dice (2 1/2 to 3 cups)

1/2 cup dried cranberries (or substitute golden raisins)

1 cup sherry vinegar

1 cup brown sugar

1 cup cranberry juice

Juice and grated zest of 1 orange

1 jalapeño or other small fresh chile of your choice, minced

3 tablespoons peeled, grated fresh ginger

1 teaspoon ground cloves

In a large nonreactive bowl, combine the rhubarb with salt. Mix well and let stand for 1 hour. Drain the rhubarb, then rinse and drain it again. Set aside.

In a large sauté pan over medium-high heat, heat the oil until hot but not smoking. Add the onions and sauté, stirring, until they are light brown, 11 to 13 minutes. Sprinkle with the dried cranberries, and set aside to cool.

In a medium nonreactive saucepan, combine the vinegar, brown sugar, cranberry juice, and orange juice and bring just to a simmer over medium-high heat, stirring once or twice to dissolve the sugar. Add the orange zest, jalapeño, ginger, and cloves, bring back to a simmer, and then remove from the heat.

Add the cooled onions and cranberries to the rhubarb and pour the hot syrup on top. Allow to cool to room temperature, uncovered, then cover and refrigerate.

This pickle will keep, covered and refrigerated, for several months.

One of the earliest edibles to show up at Westport farm stands in the spring is rhubarb. Although many folks are puzzled about what to do with this plant, it actually has many uses. It helps if you think of it as the closest thing to lemons that we can grown in the North.

In this unique, flavorful, and delicious pickle, the sourness of the rhubarb is slightly reinforced with vinegar and cranberry juice and then counteracted by several sweet ingredients—caramelized onions, brown sugar, and orange juice—to create that wonderful sweet/sour taste experience.

This recipe owes thanks to Maureen Bennett, pastry chef at the Back Eddy, who helped Dan solve the problem of the rhubarb's turning mushy when cooked. Maureen discovered that pouring hot syrup over pre-salted rhubarb results in good texture as well as good taste, giving our pickle the chutneylike consistency we were looking for.

Like lemons, this pickle works fantastically well with fish; at the Back Eddy we like to purée some of it into a jam and drizzle it over soft-shelled crabs. It is also excellent with pork, and it pleasantly surprised the palates of folks at a spring cookout last year, who were expecting only the usual condiments on their hotdogs, burgers, and chicken.

Pickled Grapes and Jicama with Celery Seed [Yield: About 6 cups]

1 cup distilled white vinegar

1 1/2 cups cider vinegar

1/2 cup white grape juice

1 cup white sugar

1/2 cup brown sugar

1 teaspoon celery seed, bruised with a rolling pin

3/4 teaspoon ground turmeric

2 teaspoons yellow mustard seed, slightly crushed with that same rolling pin

7 whole cloves

1 teaspoon salt

Piece of fresh ginger the size of your little finger, peeled and cut into rounds about the thickness of a dime

3 red or green jalapeño peppers or other small chiles of your choice, thinly sliced

4 cups red and/or green seedless grapes

1 medium jicama, peeled and cut into cubes about 3/8 inch thick (about 2 cups)

In a large, nonreactive saucepan, combine the vinegars, grape juice, white and brown sugars, celery seed, turmeric, mustard seed, cloves, and salt, and bring to a boil over medium-high heat. Turn the heat to low and simmer for 3 minutes, stirring several times to dissolve the sugars.

Remove from the heat, add all the remaining ingredients, and mix well to combine. Cool to room temperature, then cover and refrigerate. These pickles will keep, covered and refrigerated, for 2 to 3 months.

We love this combination for its appearance and textural contrasts as well as for its flavors. The crunchy texture of the jicama is perfect next to the grapes; it also can provide a pleasant surprise to those who don't know exactly what's in this pickle. The cream-colored chunks quickly take on some yellow color from the turmeric, so people think they're about to bite into a piece of pineapple, and then they get that great jicama crunch.

Serve this pickle with anything spicy, especially chicken or fish. It is very nice with curries and spicy Asian-style stews, too.

Balsamic-Pickled Peaches [Yield: About 4 cups]

1 cup balsamic vinegar (or substitute white balsamic)

3/4 cup sweet vermouth (or substitute dry vermouth)

1 cup pineapple juice

8 small peaches, pitted and cut into 6 to 8 wedges each

In a nonreactive saucepan, combine the vinegar, vermouth, and pineapple juice and bring to a boil over high heat. Add the peaches and immediately remove the pan from the heat. Allow to cool to room temperature, uncovered, then cover and refrigerate.

These pickles will develop a very nice flavor within an hour or two of cooling, but they are better if left for 48 hours before eating. They will keep, covered and refrigerated, for up to 6 weeks.

This pickle lodges itself squarely in the middle of the Italian tradition of serving fruits with a dash of balsamic vinegar. We find peaches and balsamic vinegar to be an especially wonderful combination; the musky sweetness of the peaches provides a perfect counterpoint to the smoky, sour flavor of the vinegar.

If you want your pickles to have a lighter, more peachy color, you can substitute white balsamic vinegar and dry vermouth.

Serve these luscious pickles alongside any meat, particularly roast pork or lamb.

Balsamic-Pickled Grapefruit with Shaved Fennel [Yield: About 7 cups]

1 medium fennel bulb, "shaved" lengthwise into thin slices (about 1 1/2 cups)

1 3/4 cups balsamic vinegar, plus more to taste

1/2 cup cranberry juice

1/2 cup anisette or other licorice-flavored liqueur (or substitute another 1/2 cup cranberry juice)

1 1/2-inch piece of fresh ginger as thick as your thumb, peeled and cut into thin disks

1 teaspoon whole cloves

1 teaspoon fennel seed

1/2 cup brown sugar

3 small to medium grapefruits

Put the sliced fennel into a large, non-reactive bowl and set aside.

In a nonreactive saucepan, combine the vinegar, cranberry juice, anisette, ginger, cloves, fennel seed, and brown sugar, and bring to a boil over medium-high heat. Turn the heat to low and simmer for 3 minutes, stirring once or twice to dissolve the sugar. Pour the hot syrup over the fennel and set aside to cool.

While the fennel mixture is cooling, peel and section the grapefruits over a bowl to collect the juices, removing the seeds (see note). Add the grapefruit sections with their juice to the cooled fennel and mix well. Add additional balsamic vinegar to taste. Cover and refrigerate.

This pickle will keep, covered and refrigerated, for about 10 days.

Note: There is no need to remove the membranes from the individual grapefruit sections unless you want to. Actually, even if you want to, we don't recommend it. The membranes serve to keep the sections intact in the pickling liquid, and the liquid seeps into the fruit very nicely even with the membranes intact.

A simpler version of this recipe began for Dan several Februarys ago when his folks couldn't resist a deal on a crate of grapefruit as they headed back north from Florida. They ate as many as possible en route and insisted on bestowing the rest on Dan and his wife Chris. They in turn ate their fill over the next few days but still had plenty left, at which point they were forced to admit that neither time nor appetite was on their side. So they sectioned the remaining fruits and doused them with some sugar and vinegar. They not only kept well, but also had a refreshing new taste and look.

Ever since, when the crisper drawer in any of our refrigerators becomes a death row for grapefruit or oranges, we grant them a reprieve like this. Also be sure to try this pickle with any oranges or grapefruit that dis-appoint in sweetness; overly acidic fruit becomes a tasty treat and garnish once pickled.

We really like the flavor of brown sugar and balsamic vinegar in this pickle, so that's what we call for. But if appearance is more important to you, you can get a prettier pickle by substituting white balsamic vinegar and white sugar instead, and for a really gorgeous version, combine sections from both white and pink grapefruits.

This excellent combination of flavors makes a prime garnish for seafood dishes of any type. The pickling liquid is a very tasty poaching liquid for fish, too.

Bourbon Pickled Apricots [Yield: About 4 cups]

1 cup cider vinegar

1 cup orange juice

1/2 cup white grape juice

1/4 cup sugar

1/4 cup maple syrup

2 teaspoons whole allspice berries

8 whole cloves

Finely minced zest of 2 oranges

1 tablespoon peeled, minced fresh
ginger

8 apricots, quartered and pitted
(about 4 cups)

1/2 cup bourbon of your choice

In a nonreactive saucepan, combine the vinegar, orange juice, grape juice, sugar, and maple syrup and bring to a boil over high heat, stirring occasionally to dissolve the sugar.

Add the allspice and cloves. As soon as the mixture comes back to a boil, reduce the heat to low and simmer for 5 minutes. Remove from the heat, add the zest and ginger, and allow to cool to room temperature, uncovered. Add the apricots and bourbon, then cover and refrigerate.

This pickle can be served within an hour of cooling, but the flavor improves over the next 2 days. It will keep, covered and refrigerated, for up to 6 weeks.

Apricots are picky fruits—they grow only in very specific climatic conditions, they easily succumb to all kinds of diseases, they don't travel well, and they don't continue to ripen after they are picked from the tree. For all of these reasons, it makes sense to take advantage of those occasions when you find good fresh apricots for sale and to buy as many as you possibly can, because their delicate, sweet, aromatic flavor is incomparable.

Fortunately, apricots' firm, almost dry texture makes them ideal for pickling, so if you buy enough you can preserve them for several weeks. Here we combine them with rather light-colored liquids so that we also maintain much of the appearance that led ancient Greeks and Romans to label them "golden apples of the sun."

Serve this pickle with pork chops or steaks or (our favorite way) as a snack with cocktails. They also make a nice complement to a cheese platter.

Classic Pickled Crab Apples [Yield: About 8 cups]

4 1/2 cups cider vinegar

2 3/4 cups sugar

2 cinnamon sticks, each broken in half

1 tablespoon whole allspice berries

1 teaspoon whole cloves

2 teaspoons peeled, minced fresh ginger (optional)

2 quarts crab apples (2 to 2 1/2 pounds), pricked several times with a fork

In a nonreactive saucepan large enough to hold everything, warm all the ingredients except the crab apples over medium-low heat, stirring occasionally. When the sugar has dissolved and a few bubbles start to rise to the surface of the liquid, turn off the heat. After 5 minutes, turn the heat to very low, add the crab apples, and bring to a simmer as slowly as possible. Simmer very gently until the crab apples are just tender without breaking their skins, 10 to 12 minutes; expect some casualties.

Remove from the heat and allow to cool to room temperature, then cover and refrigerate overnight before sampling. The flavor will improve over the next day or two. These pickles will keep, covered and refrigerated, for about 2 weeks.

Crab apples somehow seem associated with bygone days. Maybe it's because, like quinces and currants, they are not very good when eaten raw, so they passed out of favor with the general public. But these astringent, bright red little fruits are ideal for pickling, because the sugar makes them palatable while the vinegar maintains their essential tart/sour character.

The crab apples that are commercially available today look flawless, like big cherries, and they also have good flavor. That said, though, they are pulpier and less astringent than those you might remember. If you have a crab apple tree in your yard that you bought because you liked the spring blooms, you might want to gather the fruits and use them in this recipe. Just be sure that you wash them well and that you haven't treated them with any pesticides.

Whole crab apples tend to burst with sudden or high heat, which makes the final pickles less attractive. To avoid this, we suggest that you puncture the skin a few times and simmer gently rather than forcefully.

Pickled crab apples were Doc's favorite item on the holiday relish trays of his youth, so we recommend that you put these out for any holiday feast. They're also excellent with any kind of pork—ham, roast pork loin, chops, or what have you.

Soy-and-Ginger-Pickled Green Mango [Yield: About 3 cups]

1/3 cup light Japanese soy sauce

1/2 cup mirin (or substitute white grape juice)

1/2 cup distilled white vinegar

1/2 cup orange juice

2 tablespoons peeled, minced fresh ginger

1 small dried chile of your choice, crushed (or substitute 2 teaspoons red pepper flakes)

2 firm, slightly unripe mangoes, peeled, pitted, and cut lengthwise into 8 spears each

Combine all the ingredients in a nonreactive crock, jar, or bowl, the more cylindrical and steep-sided the better. Place a dish that fits just inside the container on top of the mangoes and weight it down with a heavy object such as a half-gallon jug of water. Refrigerate for 12 to 24 hours, and then taste for flavor. This pickle's readiness depends on how firm and thick the mango slices are to begin with—it can be ready nearly immediately, but in most cases the flavor improves over the next 3 days or so.

This pickle will keep, covered and refrigerated, for up to a month.

Although mangoes are usually associated with the flavor footprints of countries in the humid tropics, particularly India, they also match up surprisingly well with classic Japanese ingredients. In this pickle, the musky mellowness of the fruit is perfectly offset by earthy soy, sweet mirin, and pungent ginger. Just to remind the mangoes of their origins, though, we also add a bit of chile pepper.

This is just about Chris's favorite pickle. It's awesome with any kind of spicy food, with grilled or roast chicken, or as an accompaniment to rice of any variety.

Pickled Pineapple and Cranberries in Apple Juice [Yield: 5 to 6 cups]

1 pineapple, peeled, cored, and cut into large chunks (reserve the pineapple rind)

About 1/2 cup juice squeezed from the pineapple rind (or substitute canned pineapple juice)

1/3 cup fresh mint leaves

1 tablespoon freshly grated nutmeg (or substitute ground nutmeg)

1/2 cup cranberries

1/2 cup apple juice

1 cup cider vinegar

1/4 cup brown sugar

1 cinnamon stick, broken in half

10 whole cloves

In a large nonreactive bowl, combine the pineapple and juice with the mint and nutmeg.

In a medium nonreactive saucepan, bring all the remaining ingredients to a boil over medium-high heat, stirring once or twice to dissolve the brown sugar. Reduce the heat to low and simmer gently for 5 minutes. Remove from heat, allow to cool to room temperature, then discard the cinnamon stick, immediately pour the liquid over the pineapple chunks.

These pickles are ready to eat in an hour or 2 but are better if refrigerated for 24 hours before serving to allow the flavors to penetrate and meld. They will keep, covered and refrigerated, for 3 weeks.

This is a rather unusual pickle in which the tartness of the cranberries goes up against the sweetness of the pineapple, and the highly aromatic nutmeg and mint sort of drift through it all. It has a festive appearance, too, somewhat like a fruit punch.

We also like the fact that, in the great tradition of watermelon rind pickles, this pickle makes use of a rind that would otherwise be discarded. You can extract the juice from the pineapple rind with an electric juicing machine, with one of those hand-powered mechanical orange juicers, or even by just putting the rind in the center of a cutting board and pressing down on it really hard with a rolling pin.

This is a great holiday pickle. Serve it with ham, pork roast, chops, turkey, or chicken.

Fermented Pickles

Kick-Ass Westport River Barrel Cukes

Cabbage Kimchee with Pears, Turnips, and
  Salt Cod

Morea Kim's Grandmother's Stuffed Cabbage
  Kimchee

Half-Sours, Straight Up

Spicy Pickled Greens with Ginger, Asparagus,
  and Carrots

Kick-Ass Westport River Barrel Cukes [Yield: 4 quarts]

4 1/2 pounds pickling cucumbers, 3 to 5 inches long, blossom ends removed

1 or 2 handfuls small fresh chiles of your choice, stabbed or slit twice

1 large head garlic, cloves peeled and minced

1 cup peeled, grated fresh horseradish

1 large onion, peeled and sliced into disks about 1/2 inch thick

1 handful dill heads or fronds (optional)

2 tablespoons yellow mustard seed

2 tablespoons coriander seed, cracked

1 tablespoon black peppercorns

4 bay leaves, crumbled

1 handful grape, sour cherry, or oak leaves, well washed (optional)

8 cups water

1/2 cup white wine vinegar

5 tablespoons kosher or other coarse salt

In a giant bowl, combine the cucumbers, chiles, garlic, horseradish, onion, dill, mustard seed, coriander seed, peppercorns, bay leaves, and grapes leaves. Pack this mixture into a wide-mouth gallon crock or jar.

In a large separate nonreactive bowl or pitcher, combine the water, vinegar, and salt to make the brine, stirring until the salt dissolves.

Cover the cucumbers with a plate, then weight the plate down with a clean stone, a brick, or whatever you have available; the idea is to keep the cucumbers sub-

---

These pickles are a throwback to the days when every store worth its salt had a pickle barrel, and kids considered it a great treat when they could spend a nickel and fish out a big, flavor-packed cuke to eat out of hand.

The barrel that Dan uses to make these pickles at the Back Eddy is a used wine barrel of French oak that was given to him by the folks at the nearby Westport Rivers Winery, and it's big enough to accommodate about ten bushels of cukes. Sitting in the restaurant, the barrel evokes a strong nostalgic reaction from many guests, who love to tell childhood pickle stories. One woman, for example, remembered the glee of gathering oak leaves for her mother's crock, the exquisite torture of waiting for the pickles to be done, and the way her mother always reacted with mock surprise at early raids on the crock.

Deliciously aromatic while curing, this pickle also offers a vibrantly colorful holiday gift when packed into glass jars, the red chiles and white onions and horseradish standing out against the green cukes and dill fronds. If you do have grape, cherry, or oak leaves to add to the mix, they make for a more interesting appearance as well as contributing tannin, which helps keep the pickles firm.

We'd like to dedicate this pickle to vegetable grower and pickle lover Paul Costa, whose September harvest gift of a bushel of habenero chile peppers and whose abandon in insisting that we triple the chiles in our next batch earned this pickle its name.

Eat these out of hand as a snack, morning, noon, or night.

merged as they pickle. Add enough of the brine to cover the cucumbers by 2 inches or more.

Cover with a clean cloth and store at room temperature for 4 to 7 days, taking care to keep the contents submerged at all times and to skim any foam that may form on the brine's surface every day or two.

These pickles are done when their pale green color is mostly the same inside and out or when they just taste so good your discipline falls apart. They will keep, covered and refrigerated, for a month, but they start to soften around then unless you have included plenty of grape, cherry, or oak leaves. To freshen the flavor of the brine, you can strain the solids out of the liquid, bring the brine to a boil, cool it to room temperature, and re-immerse the cucumbers and other vegetables in it, discarding the original flavorings and freshening the flavor with more of those same flavorings.

Cabbage Kimchee with Pears, Turnips, and Salt Cod [Yield: About 4 cups]

1 large head napa cabbage (about 2 pounds)

3 tablespoons kosher or other coarse salt

1/2 cup minced dried salted cod (optional), soaked in water to cover until soft

1 tablespoon rice flour (or substitute all-purpose flour)

1 Bosc pear, peeled, cored, and puréed in a blender

2 tablespoons Southeast Asian fish sauce (optional)

2 teaspoons sugar

1/2 teaspoon ground nutmeg

1/4 cup water

2 tablespoons Korean dried hot red pepper powder or paste (or substitute dried red pepper flakes)

2 tablespoons diced shredded red pepper "threads" (see glossary, page 30; optional)

2 tablespoons minced garlic

1 1/2 tablespoons peeled, minced fresh ginger

1/2 small turnip, peeled and cut into long, thin strips (about 1 cup)

1 firm Bosc pear, peeled, cored, and cut into small cubes (about 1 cup)

2 scallions (green and white parts), roots trimmed, split lengthwise, and each half cut crosswise into thirds

Korea may be the only country where the national dish is a pickle. The fermented vegetable pickle called kimchee is so central to the culture and cuisine of this nation that even American cooks who know nothing else about Korean cuisine have heard of it. Although cabbage is the best-known kimchee, it actually can be made from a wide range of Asian vegetables. One characteristic all kimchees have in common, though, is their pungency. These are pickles for people who like hot.

Korean cooks use all kinds of seafood to deepen the flavor of kimchees, as well as to add protein. These typically include dried shrimp or squid, salted fish, and anchovy pastes, as well as fresh fish, squid, and oysters. In the spirit of adapting recipes to what is locally available, here we use dried salt cod, which is very popular among the large Portuguese American population of southern coastal Massachusetts. The cod adds a real depth of flavor and a touch of authenticity to the dish, and we like it a lot. If you are not fond of seafood flavors, though, you can omit it and the pickle will still be very good. The same goes, of course, for the fish sauce.

Unlike almost all the other pickles in this book, this version of kimchee needs a week or two in the refrigerator for its flavors to really develop. You can eat it before that, but the flavor of slower, refrigerated kimchees is worth the wait.

We like to serve this with grilled pork chops, pork roast, or grilled chicken. It also makes an excellent lunch or light dinner when served with brown or white rice.

Make shallow cuts in the base of the cabbage. Pry it in half lengthwise with your fingers and then again into quarters. Sprinkle the salt among all the leaves, salting the thicker bottoms more than the delicate tops. Arrange the cabbage quarters at an angle in a bowl, scattering a little more salt on the leaf tops once all the sections are in place. Let the cabbage sit at room temperature to wilt and drain for about 2 hours, until the leaves are flexible enough to fold in half without breaking. Then turn the pieces upside down so that the leaves are in the little pool of accumulated liquid for about 1/2 hour more. Rinse the cabbage to remove the salt, squeeze to remove any excess water, and then drain well.

Drain the cod and, in a small saucepan over medium heat, make the dressing: Combine the softened cod, flour, pear purée, fish sauce, sugar, nutmeg, and water. Bring just to a simmer, whisking to blend in the flour. Remove from the heat and transfer to a medium bowl. Allow to cool to room temperature, then add the red pepper powder, red pepper threads, garlic, and ginger, and stir to combine. Fold in the turnip, cubed pear, and scallions.

Coat each cabbage section with the dressing, curling the cabbage around more of the dressing to form bundles. Pack the cabbage bundles snugly into a wide-mouth nonreactive jar, crock, or pail, and place a weighted plate on top of the cabbage inside the container. Cover and let stand at room temperature for a day before transferring to the refrigerator for at least 1 week.

To serve, cut the cabbage bundles crosswise into 1/4-inch strips. This kimchee will keep, covered and refrigerated, for at least 2 months.

Morea Kim's Grandmother's Stuffed Cabbage Kimchee [Yield: About 4 quarts]

3 large heads napa cabbage (about 6 pounds)

2/3 cup coarse sea salt or other coarse salt

2 tablespoons sugar

2 tablespoons sweet rice flour (or substitute regular rice flour or 4 tablespoons wheat flour)

1 cup water

1 cup coarsely ground Korean dried hot red pepper powder (or substitute 1/2 cup cayenne pepper)

1 fat piece of fresh ginger, about 1/2 inch long, peeled and crushed into a paste (about 1 1/2 tablespoons)

1/2 head garlic, cloves peeled and crushed into a paste (about 2 1/2 tablespoons)

1 small daikon radish, 2 to 3 inches long, peeled and cut into long, thin strips

10 scallions (green and white parts), roots trimmed, cut crosswise into thirds

Make shallow cuts in the base of the cabbages. Pry them in half lengthwise with your fingers and then again into quarters. Sprinkle the salt among all the leaves, salting the thicker bottoms more than the delicate tops. Arrange the cabbage quarters at an angle in a bowl, scattering a little more salt on the leaf tops once all the sections are in place. Let the cabbage sit at room temperature to wilt and drain for about 2 hours, until the leaves are flexible enough to fold in half without breaking. Then turn the pieces upside down so that the leaves are in the puddle of accumulated liquid for about 1/2 hour more. Rinse the cabbage to remove the salt, squeeze to remove any excess water, and drain well.

While the cabbage is wilting, make the pickle dressing: In a small saucepan over medium heat, whisk the sugar and rice flour into the water until blended, and cook for 5 to 7 minutes, until the mixture is fairly gluey and puddinglike. Remove from the heat and transfer to a medium bowl. Allow to cool to room temperature, then stir in the red pepper powder, ginger, and garlic, mixing well. Fold in the daikon and scallions.

Lay each cabbage section on its back and thinly coat each leaf with the dressing, stuffing additional dressing inside the leaves. With your hands, curl (swaddle) the stuffed sections into bundles and pack them on their backs snugly against and on top of one another into a wide-

This treasured Kim family recipe is a classic cabbage, daikon, and scallion kimchee done artfully. We say artfully partly because Dan's friend Morea has a graduate degree in fine arts with a reputation for being fussy about getting things right, partly because she grew up in a household about an hour south of Seoul as the devoted apprentice to her late "grandmom," who was regarded in their community as having exceptional skill at making kimchee, but mostly because of the artful way Morea went about making this "wedding" kimchee at Dan's home on a Sunday afternoon in early October. Dan had sought her help at the suggestion of a mutual friend when he wanted to make a kimchee for Chris and Marcy's wedding dinner. At first Morea though Dan must be totally nuts to want kimchee for an American wedding, but this version was so fiercely delicious that it was a big hit, and we've been making it ever since.

Morea serves this kimchee with plain boiled or steamed rice, next to noodle soup, or with rice cake soup. We like it in all of those ways. We also agree with our friend Steve Johnson, chef/owner of the Blue Room restaurant in Cambridge, Massachusetts, who loves to pair his cabbage kimchees with grilled skirt steak.

mouth nonreactive jar, crock, or pail. Place a weighted dish on top of the cabbage, then cover and refrigerate for 10 days to 2 weeks to allow the sourness and other flavors to develop. (But sample it sooner for a fresh-tasting alternative.) As the cabbage sits, you should occasionally open up the crock to press down the top layer, immersing it in the liquid to develop flavor.

Time will balance out the sweet and sour flavors of the kimchee, but it will be flavorful enough to eat after just a day or two at room temperature, without much if any fermentation. Serve these stuffed cabbage bundles on their backs, unfurled and sliced crosswise into strips about 1 1/2 inches wide. They will keep, covered and refrigerated, for 2 months or more.

Half-Sours, Straight Up [Yield: About 8 cups]

8 cloves garlic, peeled and gently crushed

2 quarts pickling cucumbers, 3 to 5 inches long, blossom ends removed

2 small, leafy celery hearts

2 to 4 small hot fresh chiles of your choice, pricked with a fork (optional)

8 teaspoons kosher or other coarse salt

6 cups water

In a large nonreactive wide-mouth jar, crock, or pail, arrange the garlic, cucumbers, celery, and chiles. Combine the salt and water, stir briefly to dissolve the salt, and pour into the jar. Place a large plate over the cucumbers, and weigh it down with a clean stone or other nonreactive weight; the salt solution should cover the cucumbers by about 2 inches. Cover the plate with a clean cloth and store at room temperature for 4 or 5 days, taking care to keep the contents submerged at all times and skimming any foam that may form on the surface of the brine each day. Look for fermentation bubbles slowly rising to the surface after 2 or 3 days.

When the bubble action seems to have stopped and the cucumbers have turned pale green inside and out (4 to 6 days), give them a try; they should have a sharp crunch and rich, deep pickle flavor. Immediately cover the container and refrigerate.

These pickles should retain their good crunch and flavor for 3 to 5 weeks, covered and refrigerated.

Here it is, your chance to have a real, honest-to-God pickle barrel in your own home. A lot of people think of fermented pickles, particularly cucumbers, first and foremost as dill pickles. But we made this particular version without the complication of dill. We did so to allow you to taste the mellow flavor of the brine without much else besides a hint of garlic and perhaps some pepper—and also because, quite frankly, not everyone likes dill.

Upon tasting this pickle, one friend said it was "like eating the ocean." In some cultures, fermented brines like this are drunk for refreshment. To us, this particular brine, which we call "deli nectar," makes the perfect medium for poaching seafood.

Incidentally, this is a particularly good pickle to make with kids. It's easy, and it has that aspect of magic and alchemy that kids find so appealing; they love to open the crock every day to see if the fermentation process is done. Besides, skimming the foam each day gives them a sense of full participation, a feeling that is hard for younger children to achieve with forms of cooking that require heat.

This is the only real rival to the bread-and-butter pickle for an all-purpose condiment, good with just about anything you can think of.

Spicy Pickled Greens with Ginger, Asparagus, and Carrots [Yield: 8 cups]

- **2 pounds of your favorite greens: kale, mustard, chard, collard, and/or turnip, stems and stalks included**
- **4 tablespoons kosher or other coarse salt**
- **5 small stalks asparagus, whole if thin, split lengthwise if fat**
- **4 long, thin, fresh chiles such as Thai peppers, split lengthwise**
- **4 teaspoons rice flour**
- **1 cup water**
- **3 tablespoons soy sauce**
- **1 to 2 1/2 tablespoons cayenne pepper, depending on your taste for heat**
- **2 tablespoons minced garlic**
- **3 tablespoons peeled, minced fresh ginger**
- **2 tablespoons pine nuts, toasted (see page 36)**
- **4 teaspoons sugar**

If the greens are large and thick-stemmed, sprinkle them with 2 1/2 tablespoons of the salt, salting the thicker stalks and bottoms more than the delicate tops. Arrange the greens at an angle in a bowl to wilt and drain for 30 to 45 minutes, or until the leaves are flexible enough to fold in half without breaking. Then turn the pieces upside down so that the tops are in the puddle of accumulated liquid, and allow them to sit for about 1/2 hour more. Rinse the greens to remove the salt, squeeze them to remove any excess water, and then drain well. (If the greens are small and delicate, wilt them by immersing them in a brine of 1/3 cup salt to 1 gallon water for 30 to 45 minutes.)

While the greens are wilting, sprinkle the asparagus and fresh chiles with the remaining 1 1/2 tablespoons salt to wilt them, too. Drain and rinse the vegetables, then drain again along with the greens, giving them a gentle squeeze with your hands.

While all the vegetables are wilting, make the dressing: In a small saucepan over medium heat, whisk the rice flour into the water until blended, and bring the mixture just to a simmer. Allow to cool for 1 minute. Add the soy sauce, cayenne, garlic, ginger, pine nuts, and sugar and mix well.

In a large bowl, combine the dressing with the greens, asparagus, and chiles as you would a salad, tossing well to coat the leaves. Pack or layer the greens snugly into a tightly covered, wide-mouth non-reactive jar, crock, or bowl, and place a weighted plate on top, inside the container. Cover and allow to stand at room temperature for a day before transferring to the refrigerator for up to 2 weeks.

Keep these pickles tightly covered in the refrigerator, where the flavor will improve. They will keep for about 6 weeks.

Virtually any kind of sturdy, slightly bitter green will work in this Asian-inspired pickle. Be sure to pack, snuggle, bundle, and nestle the vegetables all within the confines of a container just large enough to hold them so that the liquid covers most of them. This is what blends their flavors as well as pickling them. Note that the level of liquid will rise as the brine drains moisture out of the greens.

Fish, rice, noodles of any variety, and grilled meats are all good choices for dishes to accompany this pickle. If you have a strong taste for heat, you can also coarsely chop the pickles and serve them as a powerful tossed salad.

Oil Pickles

Mango Pickle with Scorched Mustard Seed [Yield: 4 to 6 cups]

3 firm, unripe mangoes, peeled, pitted, and cut into wedges 1/4 to 1/2 inch thick

Juice and grated zest of 2 limes

1/2 cup peeled, grated fresh ginger

3 tablespoons minced garlic

2 teaspoons grainy mustard

1 or 2 jalapeños or other small chiles of your choice, cut into thin slices

2 teaspoons kosher or other coarse salt

Dash or two of your favorite hot pepper relish or hot sauce

Freshly cracked black pepper

3 tablespoons black mustard seed

1/2 cup canola or sunflower oil

In a medium nonreactive bowl, combine the mangoes with the lime juice and mix well. Set aside for 1 hour, tossing occasionally to coat. Drain the mangoes and add the lime zest, ginger, garlic, mustard, jalapeños, salt, hot pepper relish, and black pepper to taste, mixing well.

In a dry sauté pan over medium-high heat, cook the mustard seed, shaking the pan frequently, until the seeds begin to crackle and jump and the color of the seeds fades to an ashen gray, about 2 to 3 minutes more. Add the remaining oil to the pan and cook for another minute. Remove from the heat, pour over the mangoes, and mix well.

Mango pickles are ready to eat immediately, but the flavors will deepen and mellow significantly after a few weeks. Store them for 3 to 4 months, covered, in the refrigerator.

This oil pickle is typical of India and those regions of southern Africa and Southeast Asia where Indian culinary influences are strong. Indians often pickle green mangoes, which more closely resemble vegetables than fruits, with excellent results. The oil serves both as a preservative and as a medium for distributing flavor. Unlike many vinegar-preserved or fermented pickles, oil pickles mellow in both flavor and texture over time, so you might want to give these a few days in the refrigerator before you eat them. On the other hand, they are so over-the-top delicious that you may well end up eating them all the day they are made.

Turn off your smoke alarm and really scorch those mustard seeds—that is what gives this pickle its wonderfully unique flavor.

This recipe also works well with other slightly firm fruits such as peaches, nectarines, pineapple, or cantaloupe.

This is Doc's very favorite pickle, and Chris and Dan put it pretty high up on their list of favorites, too. It is excellent as a snack, with cheese as an appetizer, or with just about any grilled or roasted meat.

Oil-Pickled Mangoes with Horseradish and Chile Peppers Three Ways [Yield: 3 to 4 cups]

3 unripe mangoes, peeled, pitted, and cut lengthwise into wedges about 1/4 to 1/2 inch thick

1/4 cup fresh lemon juice

2 tablespoons red wine vinegar

1 tablespoon prepared mustard

1/3 cup peeled, grated fresh horseradish

1 tablespoon brown mustard seed, slightly cracked or crushed with a skillet

1/2 cup vegetable oil

1 teaspoon ground cardamom

1 tablespoon cumin seed, toasted (see page 36) and ground

1 tablespoon coriander seed, toasted (see page 36) and ground

1/2 teaspoon ground turmeric

2 tablespoons minced garlic

Several small fresh chiles of your choice, whole and/or cut into thin slices

1 teaspoon crushed red pepper flakes, or more to taste

1 teaspoon kosher or other coarse salt, or to taste

2 teaspoons of your favorite chili relish, or to taste (optional)

In a nonreactive bowl, combine the mangoes with the lemon juice and vinegar, and mix well. Let stand for 1 hour, tossing once or twice to coat. Drain the liquid into a cup and stir the prepared mustard and horseradish into this liquid, mixing well. Set aside.

In a large, dry skillet over medium-high heat, cook the mustard seed, shaking the pan frequently, until they begin to crackle and jump. Add the oil and, when it is hot but not smoking, stir in the cardamom, cumin, coriander, and turmeric and cook, stirring frequently, for 1 minute. Add the mangoes and garlic, reduce the heat, and cook until the mangoes soften a little, about 3 minutes. Do not overcook the mangoes or they will be mushy. Remove from the heat, stir in the chiles and red pepper flakes, and allow the mixture to cool. Add the reserved horseradish-mustard mixture along with salt and chili relish to taste, then place in a nonreactive jar and cover tightly.

This pickle is ready to eat immediately, but the flavors will deepen and mellow significantly after a few weeks. Store them for 3 to 4 months, covered, in the refrigerator.

Typically, Indian oil pickles require a long wait for the flavors to meld and penetrate and for the texture of the fruit or vegetable to soften. To hasten the process, we briefly macerate the mangoes with some acidic citrus and vinegar, and then we soften them a bit more with some heat. Rather than use the traditional mustard oil, we use prepared mustard and mustard seed. The result is a pickle that is ready to eat in a considerably shorter time than a traditional version but still has much of the same deep, bold flavor. To give it some real kick, we also use chile peppers in three guises: fresh, in dried flakes, and as part of a spicy relish.

This pickle, with its powerful mix of sweet and pungent, is perfectly suited for any Indian-style dishes. Because of its horseradish component, we also find that it's excellent with steak or beef of any kind.

Cauliflower Pickles with Raisins and Caramelized Onions [Yield: About 4 cups]

1 head cauliflower, broken or split into small florets (about 4 cups)

1/3 cup distilled white vinegar

2/3 cup vegetable oil

2 white onions, peeled and cut into very thin slices

2 teaspoons fenugreek seed, toasted (see page 36) and ground (optional)

2 tablespoons minced garlic

2 tablespoons peeled, minced fresh ginger

1/4 cup pineapple juice

1/4 cup maple syrup

3/4 cup dark raisins

2 tablespoons prepared curry powder

1/2 teaspoon cayenne pepper, or more to taste

Salt and freshly cracked white pepper

In a large nonreactive bowl, combine the cauliflower florets with the vinegar and set aside.

In a large sauté pan, heat 3 tablespoons of the oil over medium-high heat until hot but not smoking. Add the onions and sauté, stirring frequently, until dark brown, 10 to 12 minutes. Push the onions to one side of the pan, add the remaining oil, and sauté the fenugreek, garlic, and ginger, stirring frequently, for 1 minute. Add the reserved florets and vinegar along with the pineapple juice, maple syrup, raisins, curry powder, and cayenne, and sauté, stirring frequently, for another 5 minutes, incorporating the onions from the side of the pan a little at a time as you go.

Season to taste with salt and white pepper, then remove to the bowl or another container. Allow to cool to room temperature, then cover and refrigerate for 3 to 4 days before using.

These pickles will keep, covered and refrigerated, for up to 2 months. Shake or stir them every few days to redistribute the oil.

This recipe is short and sweet. The sweet comes from the caramelized onions, raisins, pineapple juice, and maple syrup, while the short (as in quick to make) comes from using prepared curry powder, which we sauté briefly to release and distribute its flavors. It helps if the curry powder is of good quality and as fresh and fragrant as possible.

We made the fenugreek optional here, since it can be hard to find. But it is a very typical ingredient in Indian-style pickles and brings a distinctive flavor to the mix, so it's worth trying to locate.

We like these pickles as an accompaniment to grilled vegetables, or try them with some simple stir-fried tofu.

Oil-Pickled Grilled Portobellos with Black Pepper and Lemon [Yield: About 2 cups]

1 pound large portobello mushroom caps (4 to 6 caps), gently cleaned with a brush or cloth

Juice of 1 lemon (about 1/4 cup)

3/4 cup olive oil, or more to cover

Salt and freshly cracked black pepper

1 tablespoon whole black peppercorns

Minced zest of 2 lemons

4 cloves garlic, peeled and crushed

1 jalapeño, Thai, or other small chile of your choice, or more to taste

About 1/3 cup, total, fresh thyme, rosemary, oregano, and/or marjoram

Build a medium-hot fire in your grill (you should be able hold your hand 5 inches above the grill surface for only 3 to 4 seconds), or preheat the oven to 500° F.

In a medium nonreactive bowl, combine the mushroom caps and the lemon juice and toss very gently to coat. Allow to stand until the mushrooms absorb the juice, 5 to 10 minutes. Rub the caps all over with some of the oil, then sprinkle generously with salt and freshly cracked pepper.

Put the caps on the grill and cook for 3 to 4 minutes per side (or roast in the preheated oven) until still firm to the touch but not hard. To check for doneness, cut into one mushroom; it should look moist throughout rather than dry in the center. Remove from the heat and cut in half.

Return the mushrooms to the bowl, add the remaining ingredients, and toss gently. Add just enough olive oil to cover the caps. (For the longest storage and to use the least amount of oil, we recommend you pack the mushrooms into a sealable wide-mouth jar about the same diameter as the caps, then add the oil.) Cover and refrigerate.

Although this pickle is ready to eat immediately, the mushrooms' flavor will improve over the next few days. To serve, remove from the refrigerator and allow to come to room temperature (the oil will have coagulated). This pickle will keep several months if covered and refrigerated, or for about 2 weeks at room temperature.

When they are grilled, the giant caps of portobello mushrooms have a deep, rich, meaty taste. Here we extend that flavor by pickling the mushrooms in olive oil. Mushrooms, like eggplant, are very absorbent and thirsty. In this situation that thirst is good because it allows the caps to drink some lemon juice and eventually absorb the oil-borne flavors, too. Add to this the flavors of the fire and you've got yourself some real taste.

We prefer thyme as the herb of choice here because it subtly reinforces the flavor of the lemon, but rosemary, marjoram, and oregano are also very nice.

Serve these richly flavored pickles with cheese and olives as an antipasto, with pasta or risotto, or on top of grilled bread or steaks. If you have any oil left over after you've eaten the mushrooms, it's ideal for salad dressing or for drizzling on top of pizzas, pasta, or grilled vegetables.

Sesame-Pickled Carrots with Ginger Strips [Yield: About 4 cups]

2 tablespoons vegetable oil

3 tablespoons Asian sesame oil

1 pound carrots, peeled and thinly sliced (about 4 cups)

3 tablespoons peeled, slivered fresh ginger

2 tablespoons orange marmalade or orange juice concentrate

Grated zest of 1 orange

2 tablespoons black and/or white sesame seed (toasted is best; see page 36)

1 or more dried red chiles to taste (optional)

1 teaspoon kosher or other coarse salt

In a medium sauté pan or wok, heat the vegetable oil and 1 tablespoon of the sesame oil over medium-high heat until hot but not smoking. Add the carrots and half of the ginger and sauté, stirring frequently, until the carrots are crisp-tender, 3 to 4 minutes. Remove to a nonreactive bowl.

Add the remaining 2 tablespoons sesame oil plus all the remaining ingredients, and toss well to combine. Cool to room temperature, then cover and refrigerate.

The flavor of these pickles does not blossom fully for 24 hours. After that, they will keep for a month, covered and refrigerated. Shake or stir them once in a while to redistribute the oil.

Carrots pickled in oil usually take a month or so to "cure"—that is, to soften and lose their raw taste. Since we're too impatient for that, we lightly sauté the carrots to give them a head start on both of these processes. This quick heating has the added advantage of bringing out the carrots' own inherent sweetness. To intensify that flavor dynamic, we use a little orange juice concentrate or (even better) orange marmalade, both of which are quite sweet but with a saving edge of tartness. We also cook half of the ginger and leave the rest raw, which gives the pickle a dual ginger flavor that we really like.

These carrots are a terrific cocktail snack. They're also very nice with shrimp, scallops, grilled fish—in fact, with seafood of any kind.

Pickled Peaches in the Style of India [Yield: About 4 cups]

1 tablespoon prepared mustard

4 tablespoons fresh lime juice

Finely minced zest of 1 lime

2 tablespoons peeled, minced fresh ginger

1 jalapeño or other fresh chile of your choice, cut into thin slices (or more to taste)

6 firm peaches, each sliced lengthwise into 8 wedges (about 4 1/2 cups)

4 tablespoons garam masala (see note) or prepared curry powder

1 medium red onion, peeled, halved, and cut into thin slices (about 1 cup)

2 teaspoons kosher or other coarse salt

1/3 cup vegetable oil

1 tablespoon black mustard seed

2 tablespoons minced garlic

2 tablespoons cayenne pepper, or more to taste

Salt and freshly cracked black pepper

In a large nonreactive bowl, combine the prepared mustard with 1 tablespoon of the lime juice and mix well. Add the remaining 3 tablespoons lime juice, zest, ginger, jalapeño, peaches, and 2 tablespoons of the garam masala, mix gently, and allow to stand for 1 or up to 2 hours.

In the meantime, in another nonreactive bowl, combine the onion with the salt, toss to coat, and allow to stand for an hour as well. Rinse the onion well, drain, and combine with the peach mixture.

In a large sauté pan, combine the oil and mustard seed and heat over medium-high heat, shaking occasionally, until the seeds begin to crackle and pop, about 1 minute. Reduce the heat to low, add the garlic, cayenne, and remaining 2 tablespoons garam masala and heat, stirring frequently, for another minute. Remove from the heat, allow to cool somewhat, and then combine with the peach and onion mixture and mix gently but thoroughly. Season to taste with salt and pepper, then cover and refrigerate.

Sample these pickles after one day to see if their flavor is mellow enough for your taste. We find that the flavor improves if the pickles are allowed to stand for a week or so. They will keep, covered and refrigerated, for at least 3 weeks. As with all oil pickles, you want to shake or stir these pickles every couple of days to keep the oil nicely distributed.

Note: To make your own version of garam masala, combine in a small bowl and mix together well the following: 2 tablespoons ground cumin, 2 tablespoons ground coriander, 1 tablespoon freshly cracked black pepper, 1 teaspoon crushed cardamom seed, 1/2 teaspoon ground cinnamon, and 1/4 teaspoon ground cloves. This mixture will keep its aromatic flavor for about 6 months if stored in a tightly sealed container in a cool, dark location.

Peaches, which are about as close to the mango as fruits from temperate climates can get, respond beautifully to the classic Indian oil pickle treatment.

Garam masala, which translates as "warm spices" is a classic North Indian spice mixture. Highly aromatic, its exact composition varies somewhat from area to area and from individual to individual. You can buy packaged garam masala in Indian or Pakistani markets or, for a fresher flavor, you can make your own (see note).

Of course, you can also take the easiest route and just use a good-quality premixed curry power.

These peaches, with their rich combination of Indian flavors heading toward the Near/Middle East, are ideally suited as an accompaniment to any type of rice dish or grilled meat.

Pickled Eggplant with Mint and Honey [Yield: 2 1/2 to 3 cups]

1 pound small eggplants, blossom ends trimmed, cut into rounds about 3/8 inch thick

1 tablespoon kosher or other coarse salt

2 tablespoons lemon juice

2 tablespoons distilled white vinegar

2 tablespoons honey

1/2 cup extra-virgin olive oil, or more to cover

2 tablespoons minced garlic

1/3 cup coarsely chopped fresh mint

Grated zest of 1 lemon

Salt and freshly cracked black pepper

2 or 3 small fresh chiles of your choice, diced (optional)

Place the eggplant slices on a nonreactive baking sheet and sprinkle them with the salt. Let them stand for 30 to 45 minutes, and then wipe them dry with paper towels.

Preheat your broiler or build a medium-hot fire in your grill (you should be able to hold your hand 5 inches above the grill surface for only 3 seconds).

In a small bowl, combine the lemon juice, vinegar, and honey and mix to combine well. Brush this mixture onto the eggplant slices, then brush on about 1/4 cup of the oil. Place the eggplant slices on the grill or leave them on the baking sheet and place it under the broiler. Cook until the eggplant has softened a little but is not fully cooked, about 2 to 3 minutes per side. Remove from the heat, and sprinkle with the garlic, mint, zest, and salt and pepper to taste. Layer into a close-fitting sealable jar or deep-sided bowl, pack in the chiles, and add just enough oil to cover. Cover tightly and refrigerate.

These pickles, which will keep at least a month at room temperature and several months refrigerated, are best served at room temperature.

Although these pickles have a certain Middle Eastern air, our inspiration actually came from Greek cooks, who like to combine honey with citrus in both pickles and dressings.

As anyone who has ever cooked with them knows, eggplants soak up oil like a sponge. So to get some flavor into them quickly, we brush them with lemon juice, vinegar, and honey before sealing their surfaces with oil. We like to leave the skins on and stack them like pancakes in a wide-mouth pint jar.

Serve these somewhat unusual pickles as an appetizer with grilled pita triangles and tahini or with lamb of any kind.

Oil-Pickled Grilled Bell Peppers with Garlic and Herbs [Yield: About 2 cups]

4 colorful bell peppers: red, yellow, purple, orange, or a combination

2 tablespoons red wine vinegar

2 tablespoons minced garlic

1/4 cup, total, fresh herbs: any one or a combination of rosemary, thyme, marjoram, oregano, mint, or sage

1 small dried chile, crushed, or a generous dash of hot pepper sauce (optional)

Salt and freshly cracked black pepper

1/4 cup extra-virgin olive oil

For best results, grill the bell peppers whole, slowly over wood coals, using low, slightly smoky heat, turning them occasionally until they're soft and their skins have begun to char and blister, about 20 to 30 minutes. (Take care not to puncture their fleshy walls as you turn them.)

Over a medium bowl, drain and reserve the juices that have collected inside the pepper cavities during grilling by slitting their bottoms, trying not to dislodge or spill seeds while doing so. Peel the peppers, then open and seed them. Cut them into strips or sections and place them in the bowl with their juices.

Add all the remaining ingredients except the oil to the bowl, mix gently, then allow to stand for 1/2 hour. Add the oil, mix gently to combine, and serve at room temperature. This pickle will keep, covered and refrigerated, for about a month. To serve, remove from the refrigerator about an hour before serving to allow the peppers and oil to come to room temperature.

The fun and secret of the delicious flavor of these smoky peppers is partly in their slow grilling, but faster grilling works too, because some of their smoky flavor comes from the charring of their skins. Bell peppers work well because their thick flesh withstands heat long enough to take on the flavors of the fire and contains enough moisture to puddle up inside. The mellow juice captured from the cavities is enlivened by just a little vinegar along with garlic and fresh herbs. This same approach can be adapted to other firm vegetables such as zucchini or onions.

These pickles obviously have dozens of culinary uses. Use them as part of an antipasto platter, on top of crostini, on pizza, puréed on pasta, or in a sandwich with fresh mozzarella.

"Supercharging" Olives

The three recipes that follow are not, strictly speaking, for pickles. Olives that you buy in the store have already been pickled, either in brine or in oil, as part of the process of removing the oleuropein that makes them inedible in their fresh state. So what we're talking about here is enlarging the flavor of something that's already pickled.

Part of the reason we're sneaking these recipes in here is that Dan is an olive fanatic. When he was just a baby, his mother fed him firm, shiny, cured, purplish-black olives "straight up" until he was strong enough to squeeze them between the folds of bite-sized pieces of Lebanese bread, which absorbed the juice. His addiction to this combination earned him the nickname "Zeithoon" (olive) when he was about six.

Another reason we're including these recipes, even though they are not quick pickling recipes, is that they are part of an old tradition followed all around the rim of the Mediterranean of charging olives to give them additional flavors.

And if those reasons aren't enough, there's still the best one of all: They taste great. All in all, supercharging olives with other flavors is a good technique to have in your repertoire.

Supercharged Cracked Green Olives with Orange and Fennel [Yield: About 2 cups]

1 pound cracked green olives

2 teaspoons frozen orange juice concentrate or orange marmalade

2 tablespoons red wine vinegar

Julienned zest of 1 orange

2 cloves garlic, peeled and minced

2 or 3 fennel fronds, coarsely chopped (about 2 tablespoons)

1 teaspoon fennel seed

1 teaspoon dried or minced fresh red chiles, or more to taste

1 teaspoon of your favorite hot relish, or more to taste (optional)

2 tablespoons extra-virgin olive oil

Rinse the olives well and dry them with a cloth or paper towel.

In a medium mixing bowl, combine the orange juice concentrate and the vinegar and mix well. Add all the remaining ingredients except the oil and toss gently. Cover and refrigerate for at least 1 hour or overnight.

Remove the olives from the refrigerator, add the oil, toss gently, then re-cover and refrigerate. Remove from the refrigerator about 1 hour before serving, to allow the olives to come to room temperature. These will keep, covered and refrigerated, for about 2 months; toss them every couple of days to redistribute the oil.

Green olives are picked when they are fully grown but not yet fully ripe. As a result, they generally have a fruitier and somewhat lighter flavor than black olives. But because the flesh of some green olives is quite firm, they often don't absorb marinades and flavors as well as their riper cousins. Cracked green olives have been slit just slightly so that they crack open a bit, allowing the flavors to penetrate more fully. This makes them ideal for supercharging.

A little spicy and a little earthy, these olives go very well with grilled pita triangles and some feta cheese. You can also serve them almost as a salad course unto themselves, along with some bread.

Supercharged Black Olives with Lemon, Garlic, and Fresh Herbs [Yield: About 2 cups]

1 pound brine-cured black olives, such as Kalamata

1/4 cup peeled, diced red onion

2 cloves garlic, peeled and minced

1 small celery stalk with leaves, chopped

1/4 cup fresh herbs: any one or a combination of parsley, thyme, marjoram, oregano, or rosemary

Minced zest of 1 lemon

1/2 teaspoon freshly cracked black pepper, or more to taste

1 teaspoon red pepper flakes, or more to taste

1 tablespoon white wine vinegar

1 tablespoon olive oil

Rinse the olives well and pat them dry with a cloth or paper towel. In a medium bowl, combine the olives with all the remaining ingredients except the oil and toss gently. Cover, refrigerate, and allow to stand at least 1 hour or as long as overnight.

Remove from the refrigerator, add the oil, and mix well, then re-cover and return to the refrigerator. Remove from the refrigerator about 1 hour before serving, to allow the olives to return to room temperature. These will keep, covered and refrigerated, for about 2 months; toss them every couple of days to redistribute the oil.

Oil, even the small amount that we use here, has a tendency to inhibit the absorption of other flavors into the olives. So to make sure that the flavors have a chance to seep into the olives, we combine the olives with everything except the small amount of oil and let them sit for a while, and then we finish with the oil. A sit of an hour or so is all right, but overnight is better.

These are great next to blanched broccoli or with skillet-wilted garlicky spinach with a handful of chickpeas and some feta or mozzarella cheese. They're also an excellent accompaniment to grilled vegetables, and of course you can just set bowls of them out for snacks any time. You can use any liquid that's left after the olives have been eaten to add intense flavor to salad dressings.

Supercharged Green Olives with Lemon and North African Spices

[Yield: About 2 cups]

1 teaspoon cumin seed, best toasted (see page 36)

1 teaspoon coriander seed, best toasted (see page 36)

2 bay leaves, crushed

1/2 teaspoon black peppercorns, cracked

3/4 teaspoon crushed dried red pepper, or more to taste

Minced zest of 2 lemons

4 cloves garlic, peeled and minced

2 tablespoons fresh thyme leaves

1/4 cup fresh lemon juice

1 pound cracked green olives

1 lemon, seeded and cut into very thin slices

1 cup, total, any one or a combination of celery, celery leaves, red onion, bell pepper, or pepperoncini, all cut into thin slices

2 tablespoons olive oil

Combine the cumin, coriander, bay leaves, peppercorns, and red pepper in a spice mill, coffee grinder, or blender and grind into a chunky powder. Place this mixture in a mortar with the zest, garlic, and half of the thyme leaves, and mash into a paste by adding the lemon juice a little at a time and crushing everything together with the pestle.

In a medium bowl, combine this mixture with the olives, mix well, cover, and allow to stand for at least 1 hour or as long as overnight. Add all the remaining ingredients, including the remaining 1 tablespoon thyme, toss well to combine, re-cover and refrigerate.

Remove from the refrigerator about 1 hour before serving, to allow the olives to come to room temperature. They will keep, covered and refrigerated, for up to 2 months; toss them every couple of days to redistribute the oil.

We start out this recipe by making a paste of spices mixed with lemon juice. This blends, melds, and somehow slightly intensifies the flavors of the spices. The result is the big flavor bad boy of our supercharged olives. It's not subtle, which means we like it a lot.

These olives are a remarkably versatile appetizer when served with some crusty bread or crackers. They are also the ideal accompaniment for tagines, couscous, or any other North African dishes, and they'll enliven roast fowl of any variety.

Pantry Pickles

Purple Pickled Eggs with Sweet Spices

Quick Pickled Ginger Strips

Pickled Horseradish

Quick Pickled Garlic with Asian Flavors

Quick Pickled Garlic with
       Mediterranean Flav

Pickled Cherry Peppers and Garlic in Oil

Dan's Grandma's Pickled Grape Leaves

Purple Pickled Eggs with Sweet Spices [Yield: 1 dozen wild eggs]

1 dozen large eggs

4 cups cider vinegar

1 beet about the size of a baseball, peeled and cut into thin slices

1/2 cup sugar

2 tablespoons coriander seed

1 teaspoon ground cinnamon

1 teaspoon ground nutmeg

Pinch of ground mace

4 to 8 dashes of hot pepper sauce (optional)

Salt and freshly cracked black pepper

Place the eggs in a medium saucepan with water to cover, bring to a boil over high heat, then remove from the heat, cover, and allow to stand for 10 minutes. Drain the eggs, dunk them into cold water, drain again, and then peel them. Puncture each egg lightly in several places with a fork (to help the pickling liquid penetrate), and set aside in a nonreactive bowl.

In the same saucepan, combine all the remaining ingredients and bring to a boil over high heat. Reduce the heat to medium and simmer vigorously until the beet slices are tender, about 15 minutes.

Pour the hot liquid over the eggs, cover, and refrigerate. You can eat them right away, but they will be better in a day or two. These pickles will keep, covered and refrigerated, for about 1 month.

Pickled eggs have long been a favorite of Pennsylvania Dutch cooks; they also used to be a staple barroom snack in parts of the Midwest and mid-Atlantic. In fact, they became a favorite of Chris's when he was at the Culinary Institute of America in Hyde Park, New York, where he spent most of his "studying" time hanging out at a local beer hall where eggs were still put out on the bar.

Here we add some sweet spices to pep up the flavor and a sliced beet to give the eggs an interesting—not to say arresting—color.

Put a bowl of these out when you have pals coming over to watch the game, play some cards, or just hang out.

Quick Pickled Ginger Strips [Yield: About 1 cup]

2/3 cup rice wine vinegar

1/3 cup sugar

1 teaspoon salt

4 knobs of fresh ginger, each about
  3 times as thick as your index finger,
  peeled and sliced into matchsticks
  (about 1 cup)

In a small saucepan, combine the vinegar, sugar, and salt and bring to a boil over high heat. When the liquid is boiling, add the ginger and count slowly to 15, then remove from the heat. Allow to cool to room temperature in the liquid, then cover and refrigerate.

This pickle will keep, covered and refrigerated, for up to 3 months.

Ginger is one of our absolute favorite flavors. We love it fresh, but these pickled strips have a certain added sweet-sour dimension that is really enticing. Americans have come to know pickled ginger largely through its traditional use as an accompaniment to sushi and sashimi, but we think it also has a natural affinity for grilled foods of any kind.

Use this pickle as a condiment with Asian dishes of any variety or as an accompaniment to grilled meat, fish, or vegetables.

Pickled Horseradish [Yield: About 1 1/2 cups]

1 cup peeled and coarsely grated fresh
  horseradish

1/2 cup prepared (storebought)
  horseradish

1/2 cup white wine vinegar

1 teaspoon kosher or other coarse salt

Combine all the ingredients in a blender and purée well. Pack into a jar with a nonreactive lid and store, covered, in the refrigerator. The horseradish is ready to eat immediately but will keep, covered and refrigerated, for months.

It is best eaten within 3 or 4 weeks, however, before the flavor and kick start to fade.

You might ask why, if we're going to the trouble of making our own homemade pickled horseradish, we would add prepared horseradish to it. We admit that it seems odd. But over many years of intense raw bar experience, Chris has found that combining the two not only intensifies the flavor and pungency of both, but prolongs their shelf life as well. It's a case, we would say, of the whole being more than the sum of the parts.

Chris's sister Susan will not eat prime rib without this condiment, a position he wholeheartedly endorses. He also likes it with steaks, and of course any self-respecting shrimp cocktail fanatic (which he confesses to being) has to have it. Try it with other shellfish, too.

Quick Pickled Garlic with Asian Flavors [Yield: About 1 cup]

1/4 cup distilled white vinegar

2 tablespoons mirin or dry sherry

1/4 cup light soy sauce

2 tablespoons fresh lime juice

1/4 cup sugar

1 cup (2 to 3 heads) garlic cloves, peeled

1 small dried chile, crumbled (optional)

2 thin disks of peeled fresh ginger (optional)

In a small nonreactive saucepan, combine the vinegar, mirin, soy sauce, lime juice, and sugar and bring to a boil over medium-high heat, stirring once or twice to dissolve the sugar. Reduce the heat to medium, add the garlic, and simmer for 30 seconds. Remove from the heat and allow to cool for 10 minutes. Add the chile and ginger, if using, and pour into a jar. Cover tightly and let stand at room temperature for at least a day before sampling one of the smaller cloves.

The flavor will improve steadily over the first few days as the liquid penetrates the garlic. This pickle will keep, covered and refrigerated, for 2 months or more.

In many parts of Asia, pickled garlic is a staple condiment, set out on the table as we might put out catsup or salsa. Traditionally, a young bulb of garlic is pickled whole while it still has a thin, tender outer skin, not yet having developed the familiar papery white layers that wrap a mature bulb. Unfortunately, these young bulbs have a short season and are not available commercially in this country except in very specialized markets. Fortunately, though, cloves of mature garlic, separated and peeled, also make excellent pickles.

Heads of garlic, with their outer rings of big cloves and smaller inner ones, seem perfectly designed for pickling. The smaller cloves pick up the flavors quicker, so you can eat them first (within a day or two) and save the bigger ones for later.

These pickles are good with fried noodles, mixed into a cold noodle salad, added to greens while you are sautéing them, or piled up alongside grilled pork dishes. You might also try drizzling some of the pickling liquid over rice or some fresh, crisp greens.

Quick Pickled Garlic with Mediterranean Flavors [Yield: About 1 cup]

1/2 cup white wine vinegar

1/4 cup sherry

3/4 teaspoon kosher or other
   coarse salt

1/4 teaspoon black peppercorns

1 bay leaf

1 (or more) small hot chile of your
   choice, slit up the side

1 cup (2 to 3 heads) garlic cloves,
   peeled

1 tablespoon coarsely chopped fresh
   oregano, thyme, or rosemary

In a small nonreactive saucepan, combine the vinegar, sherry, salt, peppercorns, bay leaf, and chile, and bring to a boil over medium-high heat, stirring once or twice to dissolve the salt. Reduce the heat to medium, add the garlic, and simmer for 30 seconds or so. Remove from the heat and add the fresh herb. Allow to cool to room temperature, uncovered, and then pour into a jar with a nonreactive lid. Cover tightly and let stand at room temperature for at least a day before sampling one of the smaller cloves.

The flavor will improve steadily over the first few days, as the liquid penetrates the garlic. This pickle will keep, covered and refrigerated, for 2 months or more.

We've just gotta say it—this pickle is tasty as hell. Sherry and garlic are a great taste combination, and the other Mediterranean flavors that they mix with here are a perfect complement. Once the liquid has cooled to room temperature, you might also toss in a handful of raisins. Don't dump the liquid when the pickles are gone, either—recharge it with more peeled garlic or use it as a pickling medium for scallions or garlic chives.

We like this pickle with savory foods—try it with mushrooms, steaks, chops, or roasts. It also adds a real flavor boost to polenta or risotto.

Pickled Cherry Peppers and Garlic in Oil [Yield: About 4 cups]

1 quart cherry peppers or other small chiles of your choice

Cloves from 1 head of garlic, peeled

1/4 cup kosher or other coarse salt

4 or 5 sprigs of fresh rosemary and/or thyme

2 cups extra-virgin olive oil, or enough to cover

Cut 2 or 3 lengthwise slits into the sides of each pepper just large enough to allow the oil to seep inside without releasing the seeds, unless you want your pepper liquid really hot.

In a large nonreactive bowl, combine the peppers, garlic, and salt. Mix well, and cover with a clean cloth or plastic wrap. Allow to stand at room temperature for 24 hours, tossing occasionally to coat with the salt. Drain the accumulated juices, wipe the peppers and garlic dry with paper towels, pack them into a quart jar with the herb sprigs, add oil to cover, and cover tightly.

Allow to stand at room temperature for a week or two so that the oil heats up and takes on the flavor of the peppers and garlic. Replenish with oil to cover now and then, as oil seeps inside and is absorbed by the peppers. These peppers and garlic will keep, covered, at room temperature for 6 months or more.

Cherry peppers make particularly nice pickles because they have a good punch but don't overload the heat. Dan grew a ton of these small hot red chiles in his garden one year from seeds given to him by some Portuguese folks who immigrated to Westport via Mozambique. This recipe is what he did with them—as much to flavor the oil as to eat the peppers. A jar with substantial shoulders and a smallish mouth helps keep the peppers submerged and also makes them into beautiful holiday gifts.

These pickles are great with Mediterranean dishes—try them with pasta, with grilled meat or fish, or as part of an antipasto platter. We also like to chop them up and use them as a flavorful garnish on bowls of beans. But perhaps their highest and best use is as an added flavor booster on the Slim Jim sandwiches of salami and cheese that our friend Ihsan Gurdal makes. You can also drizzle the oil on everything from pasta to beans to salads.

Dan's Grandma's Pickled Grape Leaves [Yield: 40 leaves]

40 or so intact, healthy grape leaves, stemmed and very well washed

1 1/2 cups water

2 tablespoons fresh lemon juice

2 tablespoons kosher or other coarse salt

Bring a large pot of salted water to a boil over high heat. Add the leaves and blanch them for about 30 seconds, then drain them and allow them to cool.

When the leaves are cool enough to handle, stack them in small bundles of about 10 each, then roll them from the side to form thick cigar shapes. Pack them tightly into a large jar or bowl that can be covered. (Grandmas Alia and Mantura used a bowl that they covered with a close-fitting dish topped with a clean stone.)

In a medium saucepan, combine the water, lemon juice, and salt and bring just to a simmer over high heat, stirring a few times to dissolve the salt. Pour the liquid over the grape leaves so that they are just submerged. Cover with a non-reactive lid and refrigerate. These leaves will keep, covered and refrigerated, for several months.

Grapes grow wild in New England, the Midwest, and many other parts of the country, and they are found all over Westport. The leaves are very useful for wrapping numerous fillings into bite-sized bundles in ways that vary widely among the countries, regions, and villages around the eastern Mediterranean. They impart a light, lemony flavor to the food they surround. Grape leaves also have another use, specific to pickling: If you add them to fruits and vegetables that you are quick-pickling, the tannin in the leaves helps keep the pickles firm and crunchy.

You can freeze grape leaves, but in our experience the texture of frozen leaves is a bit papery and fragile, so we like to preserve them in brine. It is quite possible to keep them at room temperature, but to do so you must get into canning or use a brine that is salty enough to float an egg. This was how both of Dan's grandmothers, Alia and Mantura, did it, but in those days refrigerated space was more dear. To avoid having to rinse the salt from the leaves before using them, we like to use a lighter brine along with just a touch of citrus juice, keeping a jar filled with the leaves in the refrigerator.

Index

Table of Equivalents

The exact equivalents in the following tables have been rounded for convenience.

Liquid/Dry Measures

U.S.	Metric
1/4 teaspoon	1.25 milliliters
1/2 teaspoon	2.5 milliliters
1 teaspoon	5 milliliters
1 tablespoon (3 teaspoons)	15 milliliters
1 fluid ounce (2 tablespoons)	30 milliliters
1/4 cup	60 milliliters
1/3 cup	80 milliliters
1/2 cup	120 milliliters
1 cup	240 milliliters
1 pint (2 cups)	480 milliliters
1 quart (4 cups, 32 ounces)	960 milliliters
1 gallon (4 quarts)	3.84 liters
1 ounce (by weight)	28 grams
1 pound	454 grams
2.2 pounds	1 kilogram

Length

U.S.	Metric
1/8 inch	3 millimeters
1/4 inch	6 millimeters
1/2 inch	12 millimeters
1 inch	2.5 centimeters

Oven Temperature

Fahrenheit	Celsius	Gas
250	120	1/2
275	140	1
300	150	2
325	160	3
350	180	4
375	190	5
400	200	6
425	220	7
450	230	8
475	240	9
500	260	10